MW00800630

FiRE & RAiN

A TRAGEDY IN AMERICAN AVIATION

BY JEROME GREER CHANDLER

TexasMonthlyPress

Texas Monthly Press, Inc.
P.O. Box 1569
Austin, Texas 78767

A B C D E F G H

Library of Congress Cataloging-in-Publication Data

Chandler, Jerome Greer, 1948–
    Fire & rain.

    Includes index.
    1. Aeronautics – Accidents – 1985.   2. Dallas–Fort Worth Regional Airport.
    I. Title.   II. Title: Fire and rain.
TL553.5.C46   1986   363.1'2465'097642812   86-5969
ISBN 0-87719-048-8
Book design by Kelly Toombs

For the ladies in
my life. Both of them.

CONTENTS

PREFACE

This work began at 6:14 p.m., August 2, 1985. I was in Dallas, just sitting down to dinner, when word came over Channel 8 that a plane had reportedly gone down at Dallas–Fort Worth International Airport. Within minutes the news was confirmed and I was on my way to the scene. During the next few hellish hours I was plunged into a drama so compelling that it demanded to be chronicled in the form of a full-length book. For better or worse, I decided to write it.

Nineteen eighty-five was the bloodiest year in the history of commercial aviation. No other period even comes close. According to preliminary figures released by the International Civil Aviation Organization, 2,089 human beings perished worldwide in air crashes that year. This book does not pretend to address, much less answer, all the questions that have been raised recently about air safety. There is no real reference to the crucial issue of the impact of deregulation, no exploration of the dynamics of FAA inspection of airlines and the aircraft they fly. Similarly, I have not attempted an examination of the FAA's curious dual mandate to promote air commerce while protecting those who partake of it. These and other critical questions are left to the competent pens of others.

In writing this book I faced the danger of trying to do too much. After reflection, I decided simply to present the anatomy of an air crash—its physical, social, and psychological consequences. The idea was to tell the human story behind the headlines while illuminating some basic issues. Whether these matters are resolved by our society will go a long way in determining if future books like this have to be written.

Most of us, at one time or another, have toyed with the notion of bargaining with the fates, of saying, "Hey, take all this back and I'll change my ways, my life." Aside from my family, my passions are journalism and aviation. Walking across the tarmac toward the blackened tail of Delta 191 the evening of August 2—the godawful stench of what lay ahead assaulting me as nothing since Vietnam had—I proposed a deal: "Take all this back. Give that plane, those people, life, and I'll give You my career. I'll go off somewhere and peddle encyclopedias or vacuum cleaners door to door."

But the fates don't bargain. They only bequeath. It's up to us either to live quietly with the consequences or try, in some small way, to make sure it doesn't happen again. Thus this book.

Jerome Greer Chandler
Anniston
January 11, 1986

ACKNOWLEDGMENTS

Researching, compiling, and writing a book like *Fire and Rain* can never be a solo undertaking. Those who helped me are legion. It's impossible to publicly thank them all. But I'll try.

First, my wife and my mother. Lifemate Kathy – a more accomplished writer than I can ever hope to be – provided time, constructive criticism, pre-editing, and pots of hot tea laced with love. My mom gave me a once-and-forever Dallas base, encouragement, more love, and all the butter almond ice cream I could eat.

My father, as always, helped lead the cheering section. The value of his counsel is inestimable. My sister loaned me her car and confidence to tear around Texas in search of some basic truths. My in-laws provided first readings, vegetable soup, and precious babysitting services, enough for me to finish this thing within a week of deadline.

As a full-time freelancer, I have a couple of editors to thank. First, there's Coleman Lollar, the visionary managing editor of *OAG/Frequent Flyer* magazine. He has meant more to my career as a journalist than anyone in the profession. I am also in the debt of Joe Kane and Diana Tollerson at the *Time* bureau in Atlanta. It was under their auspices that I first covered the crash of 191.

While I was in Washington researching NTSB and FAA files and generally haunting the halls of Congress, Joe and Stacie Ellis gave me their home and an overdose of Redskins football.

As always, the public affairs sections of the National Transportation Safety Board and the Federal Aviation Administration were forthcoming and cooperative. Special thanks to the NTSB's by-now-retired Brad Dunbar. May the hills of Virginia hold for you all that you hope.

Thanks to Senator Nancy Kassebaum, Congressman Norman Mineta, and the staffs of the House Subcommittees on Aviation and Investigations and Oversight.

I'm also grateful to Kathy Brown, whose copyrighted article in the *Psychiatric*

News was invaluable in the writing of the chapter "Cocoon." *OAG/Frequent Flyer* and *First Class*, the magazine of the International Airline Passengers' Association, are also due debts of gratitude for the use of material that I previously authored for those magazines. WFAA Television, Channel 8, Dallas, gave me use of a videotaped piece excerpted in the chapter "Bodies."

C. O. Miller, of System Safety in McLean, Virginia, and John Galipault of the nonprofit Aviation Safety Institute (1-800-848-7386 to report safety problems) have offered support, wisdom, and information. Thanks to Chalmers Goodlin of the Burnelli Company, Tom Tripp of the Air Transport Association of America, and Joe Dealey, Jr., of the Dallas–Fort Worth International Airport.

Dr. John McCarthy of the National Center for Atmospheric Research has been extraordinarily patient, imparting technical assistance, information and – most important – an understanding of the nature of the beast. Dr. Ron Taylor of the National Science Foundation provided valuable historical information on microbursts.

To Federal District Judge Hubert L. Will and attorneys Hal Monk and Gerald Sterns, thanks for taking the time to make straight for a layman the ways of aviation jurisprudence.

To the people of Delta Airlines, who opened their homes and souls to a stranger, may you know only blue skies and green lights. Special gratitude to Lawrence Tierney and Jim Ewing.

To Scott Lubeck and the staff of Texas Monthly Press, thanks for taking the weekly phone calls. Most of all, thanks for the encouragement, guidance, and willingness to take a chance.

Finally, peace be to those families, friends, and survivors of 191. Without your openness, candor, and compassion, this book could never have been written. May what is attempted here help ensure that those in a position to do something – those empowered and entrusted to prevent future 191s – remember the cries of your children, your husbands, your mothers. Only then will their sanitized nondecisions move beyond the bureaucratic grays of "cost effectiveness" and assume the flesh tones of real life.

J.G.C.

Been walking my
mind to an easy time, my back turned
towards the sun,
Lord knows when the cold wind blows it'll
turn your head around.
Well there's always time on the telephone
line to talk about things to come;
Sweet dreams and flying machines in
pieces on the ground.

I've seen fire and I've
seen rain.
I've seen sunny days that I thought would
never end.
I've seen lonely times when I could not find
a friend;
But I always thought that I'd see you baby,
one more time again . . .

from "Fire and Rain"
by James Taylor

THE NATURE OF THE BEAST

Thereafter are more pleasant places than North Texas in August. The heat is a palpable, enervating presence. It shimmers off the ground, giving the illusion of moisture where none exists.

All through the day of August 2, 1985, prairie and parking lot alike absorbed the radiated energy of the sun. On towards evening, after the heaviest bombardment of mid-afternoon, the earth gave it back. Through conduction, the air immediately above the ground heated. Through convection, the atmosphere drank in the heat. It was an uneven process. Heat given off by a paved area, a city, or other vast expanse of concrete was higher than that produced by ground or greenery. This particular afternoon, from the patchwork of farmland and parking lot that is northwest Dallas County, a hot spot was spawned. Surrounded by a relatively cooler circle, the pocket of warmer air rose. As it did, atmospheric pressure lessened and the pocket began to expand. At the same time, it cooled, although more slowly than the air around it. The higher the pocket ascended, the cooler it became. And simultaneously, its ability to hold water vapor lessened. Eventually, it reached a point called the *convective condensation level,* where the relative humidity is 100 percent. The product was a cloud.

At this point, something very interesting happened. By its very nature, condensation is heat-generating. Wet your finger. Wave it in the air, and you can feel the cooling evaporation. Wet your finger and hold it still in a breezeless room, and your skin becomes imperceptibly warmer. This afternoon, condensation was operating on an enormous scale. It stoked the molecular embers of the mass, a mass that had begun life not long before as merely a benign polyp. On this summer's day the structure of the atmosphere was right. The pocket mutated into a cancerous column, accelerating vertically like a roiling, living thing. Seen from a distance, it resembled the mushroom cloud of a thermonuclear explosion. The mimicry was apt, for hidden within the gangrenous giant was a heat engine, a furnace of enormous power. The hotter the day

1

grew, the more malignant the monster became. On August 2 the thermometer registered above 100 degrees.

Land and air gave birth to the beast in private. Labor was rapid. One of those charged with monitoring such gestations was Ruben Encinas, a radar specialist at the National Weather Service's facility in Stephenville, Texas. Stephenville (SEP in aviation parlance) was some eighty nautical miles southwest of the spawning ground.

About 17:40 p.m. Central Time, Encinas broke for a brief dinner. Ten minutes before, a check of his scope had disclosed nothing unusual. The meal was brief, taken in a nearby office area. Between bites, he periodically glanced at a special Kavouras monitor linked to his scope. While useful for obtaining a general picture of the weather, the Kavouras is something of a blunt instrument. Prominent geographical features and landmarks are omitted from the display—landmarks like airports.

Encinas, a competent, conscientious technician, finished eating within a quarter of an hour. At 17:48 he took an upper-air observation. By 18:00 he was back at the scope. Where half an hour earlier there had been nothing of note, the beast was now apparent.

At 17:25, fifteen minutes before Ruben Encinas took a break, Richard Douglass too decided it was time for dinner. Also an employee of NWS, he was stationed at the Federal Aviation Administration's Air Route Traffic Control Center in Fort Worth. His job was to tell controllers when Mother Nature is going to interfere with their job.

Douglass was equipped with an RRWDS, a Radar Remote Weather Display System. The unit has a two-minute delay between what SEP radar detects and what is actually depicted. Just before leaving to eat, Douglass checked his display. Nothing out of the ordinary, not near DFW. As was the case with Encinas, no one took Douglass's place when he left his position for a break. Unlike Encinas, he had no Kavouris in the lunchroom. Douglass returned between 18:08 and 18:10. There was no requirement that he coordinate the break with Encinas.

As the weathermen ate, so did the cloud—rapaciously. No longer a puffy white pocket, it quickly turned cumulonimbus. Condensation was by now a runaway **2** nuclear reaction, as water droplets grew and collided with one another. The higher the process propelled itself, the cooler the droplets became. Some became crystals of ice. Some of the remaining moisture adhered to them. The result was hail that danced about in the mounting maelstrom until it was heavy enough to overcome the dervish updrafts and fall to earth.

And so it was that accumulated moisture—frozen and liquid—overloaded the capacity of the creature to carry it. Every thunderstorm produces a downdraft, a rush of air preceding and concomitant with rain and hail. In perhaps one in a hundred cases, the downdraft itself mutates. Although researchers don't fully understand all the mechanisms at work, one theory is that dry air somehow mixes with the cold, descending moisture. Evaporation occurs. The downrushing column is chilled even further. The colder the mass, the faster it drops. When conditions are right, it can assume the velocity of a freight train.

When the storm child smashed into the ground, it dispersed in all directions, a crazed circle of out-rushing wind. As it did, its claws sheared the very fabric of the air itself. Trees were flattened, signs tumbled, and a trailer overturned. A pair of cows grazing in a nearby meadow died when they were struck by accompanying lightning.

Had the storm's fury ended there, the afternoon would have passed into historical oblivion, simply another dog day in August. But the creature's fury wasn't spent. Unwittingly, an airplane on final approach to the world's third-busiest airport entered its lair. In its desperate struggle to live, it almost managed a miraculous escape. Later, as those few who survived the savage encounter were evacuated from the remains of the craft, one of them called the beast by name. "It was wind shear," he said. "Wind shear."

AIR CRASH

The scene at the gate was relaxed as 152 passengers waited to board the giant TriStar. In the lounge sat a microcosm of America. Once, flying was for the few, the privileged, but no more. Among those who would shortly enter the sky tunnel leading to the craft were a family of five on its way to California to begin a new life, a widow on a once-in-a-lifetime jaunt to Las Vegas, and a babe in arms.

There were also the "frequent flyers," those as much at home on an airplane as urban commuters are on a bus. They represented the infrastructure of the Sunbelt: young, ambitious, accomplished. Six IBM employees and their families were returning home from a business trip. Among them was the man credited with developing the company's phenomenally successful personal computer. The vice-president of the San Antonio Mexican Chamber of Commerce also waited to board the plane, as did a professor, a lyricist, and an engineer.

They were there for Delta Airlines 191, a flight that would span the Sunbelt, from the South Florida flatlands to the Los Angeles basin. Enroute, there would be a short stop at a Manhattan-sized piece of prairie known simply as "DFW"–the Dallas–Fort Worth International Airport.

Commanding 191 this humid August day was Edward M. "Ted" Connors, one of Delta's senior captains. His first officer (copilot), Rudy Price, was one of the bright young men at Delta, a future four-striper. The second officer (flight engineer) was Nick Nassick. When not flying the line, he taught others the intricacies of managing the sophisticated trijet. Together, the three men had 42,300 hours of flying experience. They represented the elite of a demanding profession.

When the crew reported for duty at 15:10 (3:10 p.m.) Eastern Time, they were given a standard packet of forms that attested to the health of their airplane and the weather they should expect. There was only one mechanical glitch: the first-class cabin movie system didn't work. Otherwise, N726DA, a 302-passenger

5

Lockheed L1011, was ready to go. The weather at DFW was reported as "good," with scattered clouds at 6,000 feet and 12 miles of visibility. Cumulus clouds were noted to the northeast and southwest and north of the airport. Although forecast conditions at DFW were classed as "NF" (No Factor), there was a mention of possible widely scattered thundershowers becoming isolated after 20:00 (8 p.m.) Central Time.

Flight 191 departed Fort Lauderdale on schedule at 16:10 Eastern Time and raced the sun westward.

The man in seat 41J was in a hurry to get back to his wife and kids. If there is a typical frequent flyer, thirty-five-year-old Johnny Meier was one. District manager for a wholesale grocery chain, Meier sometimes thought that he lived on airplanes. He was on his way home to Temple in Central Texas, having been in South Florida for two weeks helping set up distribution routes. An associate had suggested that they fly home together via Atlanta, but Meier said no; he wanted to take 191. It was virtually a straight shot home. There would be only one connection, at DFW with a Rio Airways commuter plane.

Every time he flew, the soft-spoken Meier tried to book a window seat. There was something about the view—something magnificent—such that even after tens of thousands of miles encapsulated in an aluminum cocoon at 35,000 feet, he still got a kick out of it. Even over the flat, alluvial plains of Louisiana, nature was an artist. Bayous became silver crescents glinting in the afternoon sun. Farmland was a rich swirl of earth tones. And there was always the sky: robin's-egg blue at cruising altitude, pale chalk below, and, at the borders of the imagination, cobalt above.

On this day, Meier alternated contemplation of the heavens with bites of roast beef sandwich and swigs of Sprite from a plastic cup. While fitting the profile of a frequent flyer in many ways, Meier differs in a couple of respects. He says a silent prayer before each takeoff and he doesn't drink 'til he's back on the ground. Altitude potentiates the effects of alcohol. Should a crash ever occur, he wanted to have his wits about him.

6   Scheduled arrival time for 191 at DFW was 5:52 p.m. (17:52) Central Time. For most of the route, the flight was smooth. "I guess three-fourths of the way there, we had to put on our seatbelts because it got a little bumpy," remembers Meier. "Nothing unusual. I guess it lasted maybe two or three minutes."

While the choppiness meant nothing to Meier, it disturbed a young businessman a few rows forward. Flight attendant Wendy Robinson leaned over, assuring him that everything would be all right. The snack trays had been collected by now as the TriStar streaked towards DFW. This was the good part of the job, a chance to get to know the passengers and use subtle skills. Nearby, a woman was traveling with two young boys. The youngest had to go to the restroom. Robinson smiled and kept the four-year-old company until they returned. The young boy told her he was on his way to Dallas to visit an aunt.

One ninety-one was almost precisely half full this Friday afternoon. This gave flight attendant Vicki Foster Chavis a chance to meet some of her charges, too. Seated near the bulkhead in C Zone (the third of four passenger sections in the TriStar) was a family of five. Nearby, two young girls talked animatedly about a sorority function. At a window seat around row 27 or 28, there was a youngster traveling alone. Chavis paused to say hello. Such was the easy ambience of an altogether unremarkable passage.

Up front, Connors and Price were watching the weather – not the supposedly good conditions at DFW itself, but a line of weather along the Texas-Louisiana Gulf Coast. It was growing in intensity. Connors decided to alter 191's course and head into DFW via a more northerly arrival route. It would mean a ten- to fifteen-minute delay as the L1011 circled Texarkana; so be it. He was not one to trifle with heavy weather.

Meier remembers Connors's message over the public-address system: "He said we were seventy miles east of Dallas, and we were going to be in this holding position. He said the traffic was backing up at DFW. He was doing a little sight-seeing for us." As the giant blue and white airliner lazily orbited Northeast Texas, Connors pointed out landmarks, cities, and rivers. The passengers might be late, but he was going to do his best to make sure they enjoyed the wait. "He was trying to make a nice flight of it," says Meier. "And it was nice. A nice, enjoyable flight."

Meier eased his seat back, staring out the window at the serpentine Red River below. "I knew when I got to Dallas I had a two-hour layover, so I was going to grab something to eat. I was just hoping my wife would be there in Temple. We live about three miles from the airport. I always liked her to be there early with the kids so they could see me get off the plane. I was thinking about whether I had time to get up a golf game. I knew I wouldn't be flying out [again] until at least Sunday afternoon." Family. Friends. Golf. The tension of the past weeks melted into the haze of a summer afternoon.

At 17:43:45 Central Time, the Fort Worth Air Route Traffic Control Center called 191. In the center, shirtsleeved controllers worked in an elongated, darkened room. As they hunched over radar screens, clockwise sweeps of golden wands illuminated alphanumeric data blocks. Each tiny, creeping block represented an airplane, an aggregation of human beings held aloft by the miracle of lift. At a glance, a controller could determine the airline, type of plane, altitude, speed, and assigned altitude. Gone were the familiar "blips" of earlier, less sophisticated times.

Linked to the scopes were computers. They, in turn, were linked to dish-like

7

radar transceivers. The transceivers activated box-like transponders on board airplanes. Each transponder transmitted its own discreet code, which was translated into the data block on the scope:

FORT WORTH CENTER: "One niner one. Descend and maintain one zero thousand [10,000 feet]. The altimeter [barometric pressure setting] [is] two niner niner one, and suggest now a heading of two five zero [250 degrees, a west-southwesterly course] to join the Blue Ridge zero one zero radial and inbound [an arrival heading from a Very-High-Frequency Omni-Directional Radio-range navigational station]. We have a good area to go through."

17:43:56 – CONNORS: "Well, I'm looking at a [thunderstorm] cell at about a heading of ah, two five five [degrees], and it's a pretty good size cell, and I'd rather not go through it. I'd rather go around it one way or the other."

17:44:06 – FORT WORTH CENTER: "I can't take you south. I gotta line of departures to the south. I've had about sixty aircraft go through this area out here ten to twelve miles wide. They're getting a good ride. No problems."

17:44:16 – CONNORS: "Well, I still see a cell now about heading two four zero."

FORT WORTH CENTER: "Okay. Head [here there's an overlaying transmission which obscures the cockpit voice recorder] when I can I'll turn you into Blue Ridge. It'll be about the zero one zero radial [heading]."

17:44:33 – COPILOT PRICE: "He must be going to turn us before we get to that area."

CONNORS: "Put the girls down [get the flight attendants to buckle up]."

Fort Worth Center "turns" 191 before the heavy weather. Rudy Price is flying the airplane. It's normal practice. Captains and first officers often alternate takeoffs and landings.

17:49:29 – CONNORS TO PRICE: "You're in good shape. I'm glad we didn't have to go through that mess. I thought sure he was going to send us through it."

At 17:51:19, Flight 191 is heading southwest toward DFW. At just over 11,000 feet, Connors, Price, and flight engineer Nassick have a good view of the sprawling metroplex.

NASSICK: "Looks like it's raining over Fort Worth."

17:51:23 – PRICE: "Yeah."

17:51:42 – FORT WORTH CENTER: "Delta one ninety one heavy [the word heavy here denotes the fact the flight is a widebody jet] regional approach control one one niner zero five." [Connors has been told to contact DFW approach control on a specific frequency.]

17:51:46 – CONNORS ACKNOWLEDGES THE FREQUENCY "HANDOFF": "One one nine zero five. One niner one. You all have a nice evening. We appreciate the help."

17:51:50 – FORT WORTH CENTER: "Good day."

At 17:52:08, Connors contacts the first of three air traffic controllers who will guide 191 into a landing at DFW. Each controller works a specific leg of the landing approach. The first position, Feeder East, is manned by Robert S. Hubbert, a seventeen-year traffic control veteran. Keying his cockpit microphone, Connors gives him a call: "Regional approach. Delta one ninety one heavy going through eleven [thousand feet] with romeo."

One ninety-one has received a transmission from DFW called "ATIS Romeo." ATIS is short for Automated Terminal Information Service – a recorded message designed to tell pilots arriving and departing a particular terminal what kind of weather to expect. ATIS Romeo – designating a specific message – tells 191 that all is well: ten miles visibility, calm winds, and 101 degrees. There is no mention of rain.

17:52:15 – FEEDER EAST: "Delta one ninety one heavy fly heading two thirty five."

17:52:16 – CONNORS: "Two thirty five heading."

17:53:41 – FEEDER EAST: "Delta 191 heavy descend to seven thousand."

17:53:44 – CONNORS: "Delta one ninety one out of nine [thousand] for seven [thousand]."

17:55:46 – FEEDER EAST: "Delta one ninety one heavy turn ten degrees left. Reduce speed to one eight zero [knots]."

17:55:50 – CONNORS: "Delta one ninety one wilco."

Inside the cockpit, Price calls for 10 degrees of flaps. As the devices deploy from underneath the trailing edge of the wing, drag increases and the TriStar begins to slow. In the coach cabin, in sections C and D, passengers hear the process, feel the rhythmic rumble of slipstream against metal. The craft is "dirty" now, no longer aerodynamically clean. The landing regimen has begun.

At the same time, Nassick has begun to read out the approach check, a litany of switches to be thrown and instruments to be read. Within minutes, 191 will be on the ground.

17:56:28 – FEEDER EAST: "Attention, all aircraft listening except for Delta twelve ninety one is going across the airport. There's a little rainshower just north of the airport, and they're starting to make ILS [instrument, rather than visual] approaches. Other than Delta twelve ninety one should tune up one oh nine one [the Instrument Landing System frequency] for [Runway] one seven Left."

The ATIS that Flight 191 received a few minutes before is no longer valid. There is rain in the area, just north of an active approach runway – nothing serious, just enough precipitation to change from visual approaches to 17L, where pilots literally eyeball the runway, to the more exacting instrument variety.

17:57:00 – CONNORS TO FEEDER EAST: "One ninety one, out of seven [thousand] for five."

17:57:03 – FEEDER EAST: "Okay, one ninety one."

In the cockpit, the approach checklist continues. At 17:57:19, Nassick notes that the "No Smoking" sign is on in the cabin. In the smoking sections, passengers draw in a final few hits of nicotine before crushing their cigarettes in armrest ash trays. Tiny spirals of smoke curl up toward the ceiling where they are caught by cool blasts of air from the overhead vents. In the passenger cabin, too, they're performing prelanding rituals.

When the sign goes on, Wendy Robinson rises from her seat near the right rearmost exit door and walks through Section D, checking to make sure that seatbacks and tray tables are upright, cigarettes are out, and carry-on luggage is stowed. The practice is more than rote. There's a reason. In the event of a crash, passengers have to get out of airplanes – fast. A seatback sticking in your chest, or a bag on the floor, can be a potential killer when there is no time to spare. After perusing the cabin, Robinson returns to her seat, fastens her belt as tightly as she can, and sits in a brace position. It's standard procedure. In the event of a crash, flight attendants are supposed to be the best-restrained people on the plane.

At 17:57:45, the ILS is tuned and the sound of the identifier is heard in the cockpit. Twelve seconds later, Delta Flight 1291, overflying DFW from south to north, spots a budding cumulonimbus formation just north of the approach to Runway

10

17 Left. Flight 1291's visual perspective, *looking* north, is decidedly different from that of flights approaching *from* the north. From its vantage point, 1291 sees a rapidly building cloud formation. On the other side of the buildup is an equally rapidly dissipating rain shower. Planes approaching DFW from north to south are screened from the bilious phenomenon that 1291 sees by the shrinking shower. Flight 191 will make its final approach north to south.

17:57:57 – DELTA 1291 TO FEEDER EAST: "Delta twelve ninety one. We'd like to go around this buildup twelve o'clock to us [straight ahead]. Can we turn left a little bit and go around the other side of it?"

17:58:03 – FEEDER EAST: "Twelve ninety one. Twenty [degrees] left or so is approved. Call approach [control] [on frequency] one twenty five eight."

One ninety-one continues its approach to DFW.

In 44C and D, the center set of seats in the last passenger section, Marilyn and Mike Steinberg are thinking ahead to their California vacation. The middle-aged couple from Miami – one widowed, the other divorced – had met five and a half years before through a dating service. The first time Mike came calling, they went to the bandstand in Hollywood, Florida. There was a concert – big bands. They danced beneath the moonlight to the strains of Miller and Basie. Later, like a couple of kids, they walked along the beach. "There is a Jewish expression," smiles Marilyn Steinberg – "*Beshert:* it was meant to be." After the date, "I asked him to come in and have some iced tea. He looked up and said, 'You know, I think it's *beshert.*' I laughed." They were married a year and a half later.

He is an insurance salesman, she an artist. Just before leaving Florida, Marilyn gave her framer two works for finishing. "What Marilyn does," says Mike, "is take fabric, either quilts it, embroiders it, or both. Then, she paints it or dyes it. After that, she puts it into a shape. You could call it a soft sculpture." One of the two pieces, "Upward Bound," was particularly striking. "Most of my works, even though I may plan them beforehand, never come out the way I want them to." From the beginning, this one seemed to take on a life of its own. And the form it took, in tones of mauve and pink, was of flight. After they returned from California she planned to pick up the piece and take it to a museum for showing. But that was in a few days. For now, there was vacation and freedom from routine. Enjoy.

11

17:59:37 – FEEDER EAST: "Delta one ninety one turn right heading three four zero. Contact approach [the Arrival One controller] [on frequency] one one nine four."

17:59:42 – CONNORS: – "Three four zero [degrees]. Nineteen four [frequency]. So long, thanks for the help."

At 17:59:44, two seconds after Connors switched frequencies, Feeder East broadcast: "The wind's zero six zero [degrees] at two [knots] and we are showing gusts to sixteen. There's a little bitty thunderstorm sitting right on the final [approach to Runway 17L]. It looks like a little rain shower."

 A thunderstorm. The ATIS had said nothing about rain, much less a thunderstorm. Neither Connors nor Price heard the new report from Feeder East. From their perspective, it was just what they were told earlier: "A little rain shower just north of the airport."

17:59:47 – PRICE TO CONNORS: "We're gonna get our airplane washed."

17:59:50 – CONNORS: "What?"

17:59:51 – PRICE: "We're gonna get our airplane washed."

It wasn't the shower that Johnny Meier saw, but something off to the right side. "I was sitting on the right side of the plane. I told the people behind me, 'It sure does look like a dust storm out there, or heavy rain.' Because it was solid black. It looked like it was always to the right of us." The woman behind him "was getting kind of scared. I turned around and told her, 'Don't worry about it. There won't be a problem. Planes always take off and land in the rain.' "

17:59:54 – CONNORS TO ARRIVAL ONE CONTROLLER THOMAS WAYSON: "Approach. Delta one ninety one with ya at five [thousand feet]."

17:59:57 – ARRIVAL ONE: "One ninety one heavy, expect [to land on] one seven Left."

17:59:59 – PRICE: "Thank you, sir."

18:00:21 – ARRIVAL ONE: "Delta one ninety one heavy, fly heading of three five zero [degrees]."

18:00:24 – CONNORS: "Roger."

There are three airplanes preceding 191 on final to 17L: a Delta Boeing 737 (Flight 1061), an American Airlines 727 (Flight 351) and a corporate Learjet (N715JF). At 18:00:38, Arrival One asks the American flight: "American three fifty one, do you see the airport yet?"

18:00:38–AMERICAN 351: "As soon as we break out of this rain shower we will."

18:00:40–ARRIVAL ONE: "Okay, three fifty one. You're four [miles] from the [outer] marker [one of three that precedes the runway threshold]. Join the localizer [the ILS radio beam that will guide the plane to the ground] at or above two thousand three hundred [feet]. Cleared for ILS one seven Left approach."

18:00:46–AMERICAN 351: "Cleared for the ILS. American three fifty one."

Flight 191, on the same frequency as American 351, is monitoring the conversation. Connors and Price are now fourth in line to land. The pilot of the plane two aircraft in front of them is doing just fine. It's a rain shower, nothing more.

18:00:51–ARRIVAL ONE: "One ninety one heavy reduce speed [to] one seven zero [knots]. Turn left two seven zero [degrees]."

18:00:54–CONNORS: "Roger."

During the next couple of minutes, passengers in the rear rows of section B and the forward rows of C feel the landing gear being lowered: first, the rumble of the undercarriage fighting the 170-knot slipstream; then, a visceral "thunk" as ungainly assemblies of metal, wiring, and hydraulic lines lock into place, reaching for the earth below.

At 18:03:32 a Delta 737, Flight 963, has just cleared 17L after landing and is awaiting clearance to taxi to the terminal. Copilot David Davis, looking out his side window to the north, sees something extraordinary. He asks captain J. A. Coughlin, "Is that a waterspout out there on the end (of the runway)?"

18:03:33–COUGHLIN: "I don't know. Sure looks like it, doesn't it. Looks like a tornado or something. I've never seen anything like it."

Neither man tells the tower about the observation, a sighting screened from others approaching 17L by the "dissipating rain shower."

13

18:03:34–AN UNIDENTIFIED VOICE IN THE COCKPIT OF 191: "Stuff is moving in–"

18:03:43–CONNORS TO PRICE: "One six zero's the speed."

18:03:46–ARRIVAL ONE: "Delta one ninety one heavy, reduce speed to one five zero. Contact tower [on frequency] one two six five five."

18:03:49–CONNORS: "One two six five five. You have a nice day. We appreciate the help."

At 18:03:58, 191 contacts Gene Skipworth in the DFW tower. The controller mans the Local East position, the last leg of the approach phase. Connors's voice is relaxed and light as he greets Skipworth:

"Tower. Delta one ninety one heavy. Out here in the rain. Feels good."

18:04:01 – LOCAL EAST: "Delta one ninety one heavy. Regional tower. One seven left cleared to land. Wind zero nine zero at five [knots] gusts to one five."

18:04:06 – CONNORS: "Thank you, sir."

Some seven seconds earlier, Ruben Encinas, the National Weather Service specialist manning Stephenville radar, called the agency's Fort Worth Forecast Office. Since returning from dinner a few minutes earlier, he had analyzed the mushrooming formation just north of DFW. Again, although it wasn't noted on the map overlaying his scope, Encinas knew the location of the giant airport. What he found was a very strong echo. When he picked up the phone to Fort Worth he called the return by name: a thunderstorm. The forecaster on the other end of the line said he would put out the word. Six minutes later, he issued a Special Weather Statement.

Jack Williams was another meteorologist at the Fort Worth Forecast Office. His responsibility was the aviation desk. He too knew of the echo; he'd been watching the rapidly building return on a remote display unit. Still, he decided it didn't require an Aviation Weather Warning and didn't warrant calling the DFW tower. After all, there had been no reports from law enforcement agencies or surrounding communities of actual thunderstorm impact, no "ground truth." Williams, a longtime veteran of the Weather Service nearing retirement, said he didn't want to "cry wolf."

And yet, at 18:04:18, an airplane was on the threshold of the lair:

PRICE: "Lightning coming out of that one [cloud]."

18:04:19 – CONNORS: "What?"

18:04:21 – PRICE: "Lightning coming out of that one."

18:04:22 – CONNORS, LOOKING UP FROM THE INSTRUMENT PANEL: "Where?"

18:04:23 – PRICE: "Right ahead of us."

When Rufus Lewis turned his Learjet on final approach, he saw "nothing that alarmed him" ahead. As he continued down the ILS glideslope to 17L, turbulence began. The rain became extremely heavy, the world in front of the windscreen opaque. In an instant, his airspeed plummeted from 150 knots to 125 knots. The airplane fell. Lewis pushed the power levers forward and climbed, adding speed. He "had his hands full." And yet, he said nothing to the tower.

The lightning flash was the moment of decision for Ted Connors. We'll never know what went on in the man's mind, but, without too much conjecture, we can conclude that it is likely he did what any good pilot would. He weighed the evidence: others, right in front of him, had gone through the shower with no apparent problem; there were no reports of thunderstorms from the ground; Gene Skipworth had just cleared him to land. One ninety-one flew on.

The ride becomes bumpy. Johnny Meier sees rivulets of rain form a horizontal screen out the window of 41J. The lady behind him isn't getting any calmer. He turns around again to reassure her. They're over Grapevine Lake. "It won't be long now, 'cause when you take off and land [at DFW] you always see these two lakes. Don't worry about it. We're almost there now."

Just after 18:05, something strange begins to happen: a subtle, then sudden, mutation in airspeed. One ninety-one has been instructed to maintain 150 knots so as not to nudge too close to the Lear ahead. But the indicated airspeed is rising. No one is pushing the power levers forward; it's happening all by itself. By 18:05:07, it has ballooned to 157.46 knots. Eight seconds later, it's 162.42. Three seconds after that, at 18:05:18, IAS peaks at 173.20. Something's screwy. Connors's eyes are riveted on the indicator. Tick, tick—it flickers and drops to 171.65 knots. Flight 191 is 754 feet above the ground. The time is 18:05:19:

CONNORS TO PRICE: "Watch your speed."

A second later, the deluge begins. What has come before was mere precipitation. Now, the L1011's thin aluminum skin reverberates to the cacaphonous beat of some unholy tattoo.

18:05:21—CONNORS TO PRICE: "You're gonna lose it [airspeed] all of a sudden. There it is."

15

Rudy Price's left hand grips the power levers, urging them forward. At the same time, the nose pitches up. One ninety-one is trying to climb. And yet, the altimeter unwinds. Inexorably. By 18:05:26, they are 699 feet above Texas and closing, the speed a dangerously low 137.88 knots. The airplane damn well better start responding soon because it's beginning to flirt with stall speed, the point at which this machine will simply cease to fly.

CONNORS: "Push it [the power] up. Push it way up."

The urging becomes more insistent, rising with the crescendo of the rain: "Way up. Way up. Way up!"

By 18:05:29, the L10's three Rolls Royce turbofans are screaming—gobbling up air, compressing it, heating it, expelling it back into the turbulent heavens from whence it came. The idea is to build thrust. Speed. Life-giving, God-blessed *speed.*

In the passenger cabin, the world is a darkened, roiling absurdity. Passengers grip armrests, hands, heads, each other, in white-knuckled, vise-like panic. "The plane really started rocking sideways," remembers Johnny Meier.

By 18:05:30, the airspeed starts to creep back up. Two seconds earlier, it had apparently bottomed at 129.36. Now it's 133.60.

CONNORS: "That's it."

The altitude: 635 feet above ground level, still falling, to be sure. But there's the merest hint of sanity. For a few rational seconds, the airspeed climbs. Then, at 18:05:35, all hell breaks loose. In one second, 20 knots are lopped off. Within another couple of heartbeats, the TriStar rolls wildly to port. The left wing dips by a full 20 degrees.

CONNORS: "Hang on to the ##!"

The roll is just a teaser, a prelude to unbridled terror. The bottom drops out. From the cabin, there is a collective gasp. Flight attendant Wendy Robinson says the Serenity Prayer. Other passengers pray aloud. By now, the screech of the engines is punctuated by the isolated cries of infants and adults alike.

At 18:05:44, there is another sound, that of the Ground Proximity Warning System. Its strident mechanical message is moot: "Whoop whoop. Pull up!"

A second later, Connors shouts a single word: "Toga!"—take off go around. Already trying to reach for the receding heavens, man and machine now strain with collective sinew against forces primeval.

18:05:46–GPWS: "Whoop whoop. Pull up!"

18:05:47–CONNORS: "Push it way up!"

The mechanical voice mocks the airmen. They are losing: "Whoop whoop–." The ground is barely 200 feet away.

"There was a lot of screaming and yelling going on. I mean everybody. I wasn't really scared. I was just sort of getting tensed up," recalls Johnny Meier. "Some of the babies that were sitting up front were crying."

At 18:05:52, 6,336 feet short of the threshold of 17L and at a groundspeed of more than 215 knots, the L1011's main mounts brush rich black soil. It is a sisterly kiss. Short. Light. Toward the end of the furrow, the impression fades as 191 bounces back into the sky, only to brush the earth again.

Meier looks out the window. Prairie flashes by, then pavement. He thinks it's the runway. It's not.

State Highway 114 is an arterial road skirting the northern end of DFW, a prime throughfare for commuters between the mid-cities area and Dallas. This Friday evening, at the tail end of rush hour, 114 is busy. A westbound driver spots the TriStar some 500 to 1,000 yards to his right. It is very low, too low. How is it going to make the runway? In an instant, the question is answered. The car right in front of him, a Toyota, disintegrates. The driver dies in half a heartbeat.

"Ya know," Mike Steinberg says to his wife, "I've heard of rough landings, but this is ridiculous." The port engine ingests bits of Toyota. It's as if a giant had reached down to swat a fly and suffered a heart attack in the process. The impact slews the TriStar some 10 degrees left. The port wing dips. The conjunction of automobile and airplane dooms both.

The L10 hurdles the eastbound lane and snaps off two light standards. There's a downslope on the other side of the highway. For a second the craft skims above the ground, in mimicry of flight. Then the port wing lances the ground.

To their left, the Steinbergs see fire, then "flames roaring back." "Someone put a bomb on this plane!" screams Marilyn.

"Oh, #!" It is the last human sound from the cockpit.

"About the same time he hit on the left, he hit on the right—but a smaller version of it," says Meier. "That's when I ducked. I just put my hands on my knees and kind of locked them. I said, 'God, don't let me die. Let me live.' "

The disintegrating left wing grazes the northernmost of two water tanks near the airport's east freight area. The forward fuselage of the TriStar pivots, almost cartwheels, into the southernmost tank. In an instant, seats buckle, metal melds with flesh. Fire scourges what life is left in the forward three-fourths of the craft.

The tail cracks off as if propelled by a bullwhip and slides backwards. Fuel spills along the way, and a river of fire races to catch up.

Mike Steinberg never sees the tail shear off, never sees the carnage recede from their escape pod seemingly at the speed of light. When the tail snaps, he loses his glasses. But he feels it. Like some sort of crazy, netherworld carnival ride, he feels it. "When it finally stopped, I was on my side held by the seat belt. To my left, there was nothing. I was thinking, 'We're still here!' I looked at Marilyn and she said, 'Please

17

get me out of here.' I said, 'Wait a second and I'll get down and then help you out.' "

The tail was lying on its left side. Those like the Steinbergs had a relatively short drop to the ground, while people like Johnny Meier were literally dangling in space, held in place by seat belt and buckle.

When the plane dipped to the left and the fireball exploded, flight attendant Wendy Robinson ducked her head and closed her eyes. Her specially designed seat was equipped with a lap belt and shoulder harness. After the tail stopped, she opened her eyes: "The plane was tilted to the left. I was dangling to the left side of my jump-seat, at which point I struggled to release my seat belt. This was difficult because my body weight was on the buckle."

Quickly she changed from victim to functioning, capable crewmember, one of a handful left living. No longer was it "coffee, tea, or milk." It was, "Release your seat belts. Get up. *Get out!*" The first mandate of a flight attendant after an accident is to get passengers away from the plane. The possibility of fire is always present. Wendy's professional instincts took over. Then she saw where she was, specifically at what angle to the ground. She realized that if passengers released their belts, they would fall and injure themselves.

Johnny Meier felt the same way: "I said to myself, 'Man, I lived through this. I ain't gonna break my neck falling.' " He saw "the stewardess leave her seat and kind of crawl down some seats. So I did the same thing." There was a row hanging virtually vertically. Meier used it like a ladder. When he got to the last seat, he jumped the remaining fifteen feet or so. "When I hit the ground, I just buckled. It was a pretty good fall."

When Meier hit the ground, he immediately noticed the wind. So did the Steinbergs. It was an ill wind, and it was blowing from the north. "As I was going down ⋅[to the ground] there were bodies going by me, debris going by me. It was *flying* by me." The source of the ghastly airborne effluent was the forward part of the plane, still burning despite being drenched by thousands of gallons of water from the breached southern tank.

Aside from the wind, it was quiet—"absolutely quiet," remembers Marilyn. Meier recalls the same sensation. There were no more screams, no more crying babies. Nothing.

Then the sirens began. And so did the rain. It came in horizontal torrents, lashing the few pitiful survivors who struggled, crawled, and were carried from the tail carcass. Meier and two other male passengers who had been sitting nearby collected themselves and started back toward the tail in search of other survivors. "I saw one woman," says Meier, "[who had been] sitting on the opposite side of the plane from where I was. She was crawling out from under the plane. She had a great big old gash on her head and was bleeding. I took my handkerchief out and held it up to her head. There was another lady to the left of the plane. She was trying to crawl away. Her legs were banged up real bad. She was crying, in a lot of pain.

"I got over to this girl, and about that time the hail started coming down—marble sized. I picked up some insulation from the plane, about two feet by four feet, and held it over her upper body. She was saying, 'It hurts, it hurts.' " Meier stayed with the young woman, shielding her from the storm. "She kept on saying, 'Hold my hand. I don't want to die. Don't let me die.' "

Rescuers had been on the scene for a few minutes. "It looked like the ambulance and fire trucks were already out there waiting for the crash," says Meier. "I couldn't believe it—they got there so fast. We kept yelling, 'Come over here. We need help, too.' But no one was hearing us." The reason was the rain. "The sky was blacker. The rain—it looked like it was harder than you *ever saw* rain. It felt like it was 30 degrees outside. Everything was going in slow motion."

While Johnny Meier's improvised rescue team was combing the wreckage, Wendy Robinson was leading others away from the scene. Mike Steinberg says, "There weren't that many people who were walking around." By now the rain had washed the fuel from his eyes. Although his glasses were gone, he could still make out what was happening to the north. "I'm standing in the field and I'm looking to the left and I see what looked like the front of the plane. It was in flames, and the fire fighters were pouring whatever it was to try to douse it. I was fascinated." A fire fighter came along, took a look at the couple, and said, "You're okay. You're still walking." Hand in hand, the Steinbergs were led to a police car for shelter.

And shelter was needed from the demonic wind. It began to whip the airport at peaks of 70 knots. So strong was it that those few who dared to look up from frightened crouches saw something remarkable: the tail of the TriStar, virtually the only recognizable piece of airplane left, righted itself with an agonized groan.

After the gusts subsided, Meier managed to carry half a dozen people to waiting ambulances. "You don't know how you're going to react to something like that until it hits you," he says quietly. After he had searched the tail, he headed toward the water towers. "I didn't want to leave anybody that was out there that was injured and just couldn't cry for help. I wanted to make sure I looked everywhere I could that people might be. You know, you always see it on TV that somebody got left behind. I didn't want it to haunt my memories that I left somebody that could've lived if I'd found them."

On the path toward the tanks were scattered pieces of passenger cabin, remnants shed by the tail as it rocketed backwards. "I walked up to this one guy I thought was all right. He had a cut on the left side of his face, and his jaw was kind of cut up, had blood on it. But his eyes were open," shivers Meier, "and he was still sitting there." The man was dead. Meier stumbled on, soot, fumes, debris, and stench assaulting him every step of the way. "I kept walking back, about 175 yards at the most, and a couple of guys – I don't know who they were, they had ID badges – asked me if I needed help." Meier said no. He just wanted to know what time it was. His flight for Temple left at eight. He didn't want to miss it.

KATHRYN KAISER

For Kathryn Kaiser, 191 was a freedom flight, the first tentative step of the rest of her life. At the age of sixty-nine, the attractive widow was just beginning to live for herself. Six months earlier, her lifemate lost a war of attrition to heart disease. Before his health-induced retirement, Bob Kaiser had been an aggressive outdoorsman and General Motors executive. In 1972 the first of five myocardial infarctions felled the strapping midwesterner.

At the Miami Heart Institute, they called him the "miracle man" as he continued to cling tenaciously to life. Kaiser was one of a series of test patients on an experimental drug, one aimed at controlling cardiac arrhythmia, a complication of his condition. A robust physical appearance belied reality. So anomalous was Kaiser's case that whenever he entered the institute, his bedside was an obligatory stop for new physicians. Still, during his thirteen-year ordeal, he was bedridden for only one extended period. This relatively normal life had as much to do with his wife as with wonder drugs – probably more. Kathryn was selfless, devoted, and almost totally immersed in her husband's constrained life.

They met when he was twenty-seven and she twenty-two. German Lutheran by birth and reserved by temperament, the two were immediately attracted to one another. This would have been acceptable in the tableau of Depression-dominated Toledo had Kathryn not been engaged to another man. Not to be stifled by convention, Bob tearfully asked her to break the engagement. The man who swore he would do the sensible thing and never marry before he was thirty took Kathryn as his bride on April 19, 1941.

Kathryn – "Kay" to her friends, "Katie" to her only brother, and "Cita" to her children and grandchildren – was described by those who knew her as a classy lady with never a hair out of place. An aristocratic bearing belied a quick sense of humor. She laughed easily, often at herself. Taste and decorum were tempered by other things, too, like a fondness for fishing. She always baited her own hook. President of her bowling league (with a 168 average) and an avid bridge player, Kathryn Kaiser never forgot a special event. Her desk calendar was a chronological compendium of family and friends, inscribed with notes dating back before her children were born.

Order and consistent routine ruled her life. She read daily newspapers thoroughly. After she finished, she carefully rearranged them, section and page. Along with this meticulous metering of life went a strong sense of responsibility to her husband and hero. On at least one occasion, she saved his life.

While she was busy in the kitchen one afternoon, Kathryn heard a thump from the den. She called Bob's name, then heard nothing. Dropping what she was doing, she rushed to find him slumped on the floor. The tiny 5'1" woman pulled his rangy 165-pound frame out flat and breathed life into him. She'd rehearsed the exercise before. Like virtually everything else in her world, the CPR course she had taken was for a specific purpose.

Before the health problems, two children were born of Bob and Kathryn Kaiser: Karen and Kandace. Although close, they are a study in contrast. Karen Kaiser Clark is an author and lecturer who lives with her husband and two children near St. Paul. The older of the two, she's a bubbly, petite extrovert. Kandace Kaiser is a South Florida real estate broker and divorcee who carries herself with the tall, elegant bearing of the fashion model she once was. Their father's illness transformed them both. They, in turn, redefined some very basic relationships. A proper, correct upper midwestern family pinioned by discipline and denial became a demonstratively loving unit.

For Kandace, with each of her father's attacks, the lens through which she viewed the world was racheted into sharper focus. As the younger child, she had revered and respected her parents. "They were really, in my mind I guess, not subject to human frailties, desires and wants. They were my parents, not really people."

It was only reluctantly that she began to see them as flesh of her flesh, something part of—not apart from—herself. "Through the years of Daddy's getting well and suddenly falling ill again, I watched my mother become emotionally spastic and helpless." The result was anger. Parents weren't allowed to act like that, weren't allowed to be weak and fall apart. They had always been the ones with the answers.

The desperate contractions of her father's heart literally squeezed the child out of the daughter. What was left was sinew and strength. She could eventually go to him and say, "What's the matter with you? Let's go to the hospital. Stop being strong. Stop being stubborn. I want you to live." Daughter became friend in a relationship that evolved without words. Because of her proximity to Bob and Kathryn, Kandace's actions were enough.

She became confidante to her mother, who was becoming more frightened and childlike with each successive onslaught. "The strength that she leaned on [Bob] was beginning to fail her. She would look to me to take the initiative and be assertive. She hid it very well, but she would confide in me that she did not want to be with Daddy when he died." For all her strength, neither did Kandace. Yet, they did not want him to die alone.

Kandace describes herself as a "horrible romantic" who was always in frilly skirts, into playing with dolls, and "boy crazy."

Karen "marched to the beat of a different drummer." That drumbeat produced two books: *Where Have All the Children Gone? Gone to Grownups Everyone* (dedicated to her parents) and *Grow Deep, Not Just Tall.* Both deal with human growth and potential; both are very much a product of her own rearing.

When she was growing up, Karen craved affirmation for her accomplishments. "I would hunger for those words. When my father had his first attack, I had never said, 'I love you' [to him]. The reason I never said it? I thought, 'fair is fair.' He never told me. My father was not a particularly affectionate person." To a smaller degree, neither was her mother. "She was a real perfectionist," says Karen, "extremely neat and quite critical of us girls in our growing up."

Those words—"I love you"—wouldn't come until deep in adulthood. As Bob Kaiser lay in a hospital bed, bound like some lanky Gulliver by the invasive probes of modern medicine, his diminutive firstborn looked down and said it. Kaiser just smiled and glanced at the clock. Embarrassed, Karen left.

A year later, she attended a workshop. One of the participants dared others to say what needed to be said before it was too late. Buoyed, she tried again. Kathryn was out for an evening's bridge game. When she was sure her mother had gone, Karen picked up the phone and dialed her parents' number in Boca Raton. After a dozen rings, her father answered. He couldn't believe she had called just to talk to him. He never answered the phone when Kathryn was at bridge because he said it was always for her. He joked that he'd inevitably get the message wrong and wind up in trouble.

Karen said that she'd called to tell him something. After small talk and emotional parry, she said it again: "I love you." That was "real nice," said her father. Glad she called. Undaunted, she screwed up her telephonically insulated courage and hit him with the family's ingrained sense of fair play. It was his turn. From the other end of the line, a soft chuckle: "The feeling is mutual." Closer than ever, Karen laughed and pressed on. Finally, Bob Kaiser too tested the words of the foreign tongue: "I love you."

A dozen years later, on January 23, 1985, he called Karen in Minnesota "for the first time in his life, all by himself." Kathryn was in Bermuda with her bridge club, a move he had wholeheartedly supported. It was the first real trip she had taken without Bob. For Karen, the call was a shock, *deja vu* with a twist. "It was just like

23

it was twelve years earlier when I called him and *he* didn't believe it." At the end of the conversation, her father said, "Say hi to Lou [her husband] and the kids. One more thing, Karen—I love you." Two weeks later, Bob Kaiser died.

Kathryn's worst fear and anguished hope had both been realized: Bob was gone and she had not been there. Kandace picked her up at the airport. "The first thing I did was put my arms around her. She shrunk and became like a very tiny person." "Mother," she said, "I want to tell you something. I only want to tell you once. Do not feel guilty for not being here."

In the months that followed, Kathryn set about, with her daughters' help, to construct a life of her own. Aside from family and bridge, she had precious little to build on. She listened to advice from friends and family. Outwardly, she accepted the notion that widows could make their own lives, have their own fun, and—in the process—become themselves. Both Kandace and Karen told her, "Go ahead. Try it. We know it feels awkward." Kathryn went through the motions, trying to make something happen. "She was doing it because she knew Daddy would want her to. But she really didn't want to." Bob Kaiser was still calling the shots. Her all-controlling desk calendar reflected the reality. It was forever frozen on the day of his death.

Painfully, things began to change. Kathryn was beginning to emerge from her husband's shadow when she decided to join her club on a trip to Las Vegas. "Of all the places for her to go!" smiles Kandace. "That's someplace my father would never have wanted to go to in a million years. He'd rather go fishing. This represented a whole lot of things that were totally different from anything my mother had ever done."

Kathryn and Kandace went on a spending spree preparing for the trip. In a single afternoon, they spent well over a thousand dollars on clothes. "We talked about how Daddy would probably roll over in his grave to think we were spending all this money so recklessly." The afternoon's prize was a chiffon dress—powder blue.

The evening before she left, Kathryn's conservative side reasserted itself. While packing, she told Kandace she planned to spend fifty dollars per day. "I sort of snickered," laughs Kandace, "and told her fifty dollars might buy her breakfast." One more thing. Did Kandace know where her checkbooks were and what was in the safe-deposit box? "I got this strange feeling," remembers Kandace. "Why were we talking about this?" "Just in case," said her mother. Kandace dismissed the thought.

On the afternoon of August 2, she bundled Kathryn off to Las Vegas. The sensation was not unlike sending a child off to school on the first day. The flight was a rather straightforward affair. Kathryn would only have to change planes once, in Dallas.

Work done and mother finally off, Kandace returned home a little after seven, Eastern Time. As she sorted through her mail, the evening news droned on.

Beruit, East-West tensions, famine, and flood: white noise for millions of living rooms across the nation. Then, a change in tempo, an unnatural pause in the slick segues of one story to the other. "I looked up at the television. The announcer was saying that there had just been a plane crash at the Dallas–Fort Worth Airport. There were signs of survivors and we should stay tuned."

Kandace looked at the clock and "got this sinking feeling." She went to the kitchen and got Kathryn's itinerary. She was supposed to have landed at DFW about ten minutes before six, Central Time. That was some half hour ago. It couldn't be. Clutching the paper in her hand, she was pulled back to the set. Now it was confirmed. The plane was an L1011, Delta Flight 191.

Everything just drained out of her, a "reverse rush," she calls the feeling. Almost catatonically, her hand reached for the phone. "Karen–Gotta call Karen." As she absently heard the phone ring in suburban St. Paul, images of fire and rain, ambulances and people running flashed on the screen. "I was frantically looking for *something* that vaguely resembled my mother." Then it dawned on her that no one was answering.

That morning, Karen and Lou Clark had left with another couple for a short vacation in northern Minnesota. Their kids were at camp. Before going to dinner, they went briefly to the hotel room. It was a little after 6:10 Central Time. There was time to kill before the meal, and Karen glanced at the television. "The heck with it. I'm not going to turn it on. Look, we're on vacation. The news is always bad. We don't need that." Good friends and good food awaited. It was time to tune out the world.

They returned from dinner about eleven. Karen pulled out the knob of the set and Ted Koppel materialized. He was "saying something about a terrible airplane crash, over 130 people killed," remembers Karen. It was the end of *Nightline*, and Koppel was just wrapping up. Neither the words "Delta" nor "Fort Lauderdale" registered. Karen, an extraordinarily empathetic person, turned to Lou and her friends and said, "Oh, Dear God. There's been a terrible accident. Think of those poor grieving families." Silently, they said a prayer. It would not be until later that they realized it was for her own family.

Karen didn't sleep well that night–"not from any premonition. I was just restless and worried about that crash. I do so much in the area of coping with crisis."

By then, Kandace had called Karen's neighbor. When the friend answered the phone, Kandace froze. "I couldn't bring myself to say what I knew had happened." Regaining her composure, she said, "Where's Karen? We have to find Karen." The neighbor called another friend. She, in turn, called Boca Raton. Kandace's mind was racing. She was also desperate to know if her mother was alive.

By then, a Florida friend had arrived at Kandace's. She phoned Delta. Was there any verification on the names? Did they have a passenger manifest together?

No, not yet. They'd call as soon as they knew something. At 10:20 the phone rang. No word yet.

Kandace continued the vigil. The Cable News Network said survivors had been taken to four hospitals in the Dallas area. She scribbled the names down and called information. One by one, she tried to get through. The lines were choked. At 2:30 a.m, she finally contacted Parkland. A chaplain checked the list of survivors, those who had been admitted not only to Parkland, but other hospitals as well. "There was this deafening silence. Then she told me compassionately, but very firmly that Kathryn Kaiser was not on the list."

By Saturday morning, an all-points bulletin was out in Minnesota for Karen and Lou. On awakening from the restless night, they had breakfast at the Grand Portage Hotel on an Indian reservation. Still bothered by the tail end of the *Nightline* report, Karen asked the waitress if she had heard anything about a plane crash. She hadn't. Perhaps there was a paper? In this part of Minnesota, they didn't arrive until noon. Karen and Lou continued their trip.

At a lunch break, Karen found a copy of the *Minneapolis Star & Tribune*. "I looked at the headline and I saw the tail of the plane." The name "Fort Lauderdale" finally registered. The flight number didn't—this despite the fact that Karen had written it down during her last conversation with her mother. Only gradually could she acknowledge the devastating reality: "My God, my mother might have been on that flight!"

In the deep backwoods of Minnesota, telephone connections don't always work. Karen and Lou drove to a tourist center some twenty miles away at Grand Marais and called Delta. Karen was patched into a marketing representative in Denver. Fifteen minutes later, nightmare became reality: "I regret to inform you—" began the disembodied voice. Karen broke down: "No, no! You can't tell me that's true. My father just died five months ago." For an instant, the line seemed dead. "Please, don't hang up on me," she pleaded. Then, compassionately, soothingly, the voice said, "Karen, I will not hang up on you. I'm going to do everything I can to help."

Lou tried to take down the information but couldn't. The couple they were traveling with did. A flight was confirmed for them from Duluth to Minneapolis, where connections would be made to DFW. The trip and lodging would be at Delta's expense. Another airline said they would hold their 4 p.m. flight from Duluth. It was the last one that would leave in time for the Minneapolis connection.

The Clarks careened around the rural roads of northern Minnesota, the speedometer pegged at 85. At the airport, they raced up to the airline counter and immediately identified themselves. "None of them would acknowledge us," says Karen. Lou stepped in: "Please, will you help us get on that flight?" Nothing. Finally, Karen broke down: "My mother is dead. She was killed on Delta 191 in Texas. We've

26

got to get on that flight." Karen stepped behind the counter and touched the agent imploringly. "He turned to me and said, 'Lady, you get out of here or I'm calling security.'" Lou lost his temper: "You must get us on that flight!"

In tears, the Clarks watched the plane leave without them.

Some forty-one hours after the tires of Delta 191 first furrowed the black North Texas soil, the Clarks' flight uneventfully touched down at DFW. The kids had joined them for the trip. Karen believes grieving should be a family affair, and so it was.

Kandace had already arrived, taking a Saturday morning flight from Florida. With her, she carried Kathryn Kaiser's dental records. It would be Wednesday until they positively identified the person to whom the file had once belonged, one of the last twenty passengers matched to a name.

Kandace and Karen flew to Boca Raton on Thursday. A week earlier their mother's condominium had been full of laughter and the rustle of tissue paper as boxes were opened and a blue chiffon dress was held admiringly at arm's length. A week earlier, their mother was busy preparing for the rest of her life. The place waited expectantly for her return. The radio was on, the nap of the rug perfect. On the kitchen table was a passport picture. Later in the year, she had planned to go to China. On the same table lay a confirmation for Delta 191.

In the bedroom Bob and his bride had shared for their thirteen years in Florida was an urn. A week before the trip, Kathryn had gotten a call from the funeral home. They could no longer store her husband's ashes. She brought them home, looked around and knew immediately where they belonged. "Maybe people will think I'm crazy," she tearfully laughed, "putting him under his side of the bed."

Together, the sisters wrote their mother's service, choosing a reading from The Prophets: "The deeper sorrow carves into your being, the more joy you can contain." After the memorial in Florida, Kandace and Karen boarded a plane bound for Toledo. In their hands, they cradled a package containing two urns. Their parents would be buried together, in the place they had met forty-four years before. Nearing journey's end, the craft descended through a summer thunderstorm. Lightning crazed the sky, and they were afraid. Together, the Kaisers huddled against the storm. **27**

ANNIE'S AIRPLANE

On the mantelpiece of a suburban Dallas home rests a large white styrofoam sailplane, the kind that hangs from the ceilings of toy stores, the kind that makes kids stare and fathers wish for a hill and a hint of breeze. This one belongs to Annie White, age eight. She is blond, bright, and not in the least bashful. Her mother, Leora, bought it for her, not at the behest of her husband but of a psychiatrist. He thought it might help.

When Ron White died, the thirty-three-year-old was sitting in the middle row of seats, left side, just behind the wing. His death was virtually instantaneous. White left behind a wife of ten and a half years, two daughters, and a world of promise.

Music says much about the man. His tape deck alternated Three Dog Night with Itzhak Perlman, Tammy Wynette with Gilbert and Sullivan. The 6'1", blond, blue-eyed Texan defied a lot of stereotypes. In a town where the fast lane is negotiated in BMWs, he chose a pickup truck.

White had just been promoted to buyer for a major Dallas–Fort Worth nursery chain when he left on his first business trip. Since the time he joined the company after graduating from Texas A&M, advancements had come rapidly – but not without a price. As a store manager, "he worked just incredible hours," remembers Leora. The pretty auburn-haired widow sits on the couch of their home. Annie leans over the back, while fourteen-month-old Dana, a mass of blond ringlets and curiosity, sits on her mother's lap.

"He worked seven days a week. The store opened at 9 and closed at 7. He'd go in at 8:30, and we wouldn't usually see him until 8 or 9. Then, there were times like spring and around Christmas – they sell Christmas trees and things – when it was worse." Her voice trails off in a half-laugh. With the step up to buyer, "it was like, 'Whew! You made it. Now you'll get to be home more with the kids.'"

Ron and Leora had known each other since childhood. They had gone to the same church and the same junior high and had had the same friends. In high school the relationship quickened. Both were drawn to speech and drama. "He was very good. I was not so good," she smiles. She liked poetry. He was eclectic: "Ronnie did a lot of different things, poetry reading, dramatic interpretation."

Ron had maintained his interest in theater during a four-year stint as a navy communications technician. After discharge, he had even landed a part in the production *Texas* performed at Palo Duro Canyon State Park. By then, Annie was just over a year old (they had married shortly before his discharge), and he was attending Texas A&M on the GI Bill. (A sign on the White's front door warns: NO AGGIE JOAKS!)

Leora worked to support the young family. While a bit of a romantic and still in love with the stage, Ron wasn't about to link his family's fate to an actor's fortune. He graduated from college with a degree in parks administration. The idea was to combine another love—the outdoors—with making a living. He held a succession of parks jobs in Dallas, and the Whites were just scraping by. Enter the business world with its perks, promise, and pain.

He coped with the corporate grind by taking deep, sweet draughts of family and music. They were his touchstones. Occasionally, Ron the responsible yielded to Ron the romantic. "If he was late for work, he'd sometimes sit down and practice piano," says Leora. "He was not only creative and talented, he made life more *interesting*—like when he sat down to compose music. Ron celebrated the birth of his second-born by composing a piano instrumental. He called it "Dana's Song." But he couldn't actually score the piece. Leora is afraid it's lost. Perhaps if she could only sing it, she says, somehow draw the melody from the shadows of the silent instrument, then—

Ron was excited about his first real business trip. In South Florida he attended a trade show and toured a number of nurseries looking for tropical plants to hang in winter windows. Leora White last touched her husband Tuesday morning, July 30. She wanted to drive him to DFW this first important time. He said, "No, let's not start that." So he had driven his pickup and parked it at the airport.

He called home every night. "He was really having a good time. In fact, Thursday night I talked to him and he said, 'Hey, I can't believe that they pay me for this! It's just a lot of fun.' " It was the last time lifelong friends, mother and father, lover and beloved, ever spoke to one another. Before he rang off, Ron told Leora he would be home the following night, August 2.

She heard about the crash while making dinner. Annie and a playmate were in front of the television when the initial bulletin broke. Annie called her mother in and for half an hour they watched, waiting for further word as to what had happened. Initially, Leora was only mildly concerned. DFW is a busy place; there's lots of air traffic, especially on a Friday evening. "He worked for so long driving home late at night and with money that I'd sort of trained myself not to worry

30

about things." Then they broadcast the flight number. "I knew it was his."

Leora called a relative to babysit with the kids and headed toward Parkland. Television reports had said there was a fire. As a medical researcher at the adjacent University of Texas Health Science Center, she knew that survivors would be taken to Parkland's burn unit.

She pulled up to the emergency entrance about seven. If Ron were alive, she would be there for him. As the lists of survivors were compiled and posted, the name White was absent. Leora carried Ron's itinerary with her. If the lists offered no hope, the phones might. "I called everywhere. There were two other men with him [on the trip]. They had different plans." One had stayed over with his wife for an extended vacation. The other was returning to Dallas via Atlanta. Was it possible that Ron had changed plans? "I thought, there is that chance that he wasn't on it." Yet something else told her he was, "because he would have called. He would have let me know."

After phoning the president of his company, she managed to get through to the two other men who were with him in Florida. Ron White had been dropped at the Fort Lauderdale airport just before 3:30 Eastern Time, just over half an hour before scheduled departure.

In the depths of Parkland, Delta had set up a center to aid the families. Leora White says that some of the airline personnel were "very confused." She assumed that passenger information was being coordinated at the center, that any word about the fate of her husband would come from there. It was not until the following day that she discovered that Ron was actually on 191.

On Saturday, she believes it was in the afternoon, the phone rang at home. It was Delta, a call from Atlanta. A person said "that they'd confirmed the passenger list and that he was on the plane and that he was not on the list of survivors. They assumed he was dead." Leora wanted to identify the body, or at least have a member of Ron's family do so. Delta suggested that she mail Ron's dental records. "Wait a minute!" she responded. "I'm not going to wait three weeks!"

She couldn't remember his dentist's name. She called the nursery to see if they had it in their files. They didn't. Then she found a dental receipt and called a **31** relative who is a toxicologist in the Department of Forensic Science near Parkland. He took over from there.

Meanwhile, another relative had gotten erroneous word—Leora says from Delta—that Ron's body could be identified at DFW. On arrival at the Delta terminal, she says the family encountered a "very unsympathetic" employee. "I said, 'Okay, that's fine. We can't identify the body, but can't you give us some information so we can help?'" After two hours of running around Terminal 4E, "what he said was, 'Give me your phone number and we'll call you.'" Although Leora wasn't incensed, other members of the family were. "I should have been [mad], but I wasn't with it."

At last, the family found help, another Delta employee. "She was really good," says Leora. "She stayed with us the whole time." The family was directed to a special room where Leora filled out an FBI identification form "about physical things, rings he might be wearing and other ways to identify him." Exhausted, she went home. On Sunday morning at 6:30 her phone rang again. Positive identification had been made.

The rest of the day was a blur. There were arrangements to make, friends to greet, and tears to shed. Later in the day, people armed with notepads and sympathy came by. Friends told Leora, " 'You don't have to talk to those reporters if you don't want to.' But I wanted to." It was a time for catharsis, and talking to a perfect stranger was perhaps the best way to go about it. "It helped," she says gently.

Tuesday, a week after Ron White had left for Florida, his remains were cremated. A memorial service took the place of graveside ceremonies. A Methodist minister and friend of the family presided.

In the weeks immediately following, Leora wore a sad, soft countenance. Anger, were it ever to come, had yet to surface. "I don't really blame anyone. I might – I mean I don't know what the results of the investigation are going to be. I don't know who was at fault, or even if someone was at fault, or–" Does it matter? "Not really," she almost whispers, and then looks down. "It matters because I would rather it not happen to anyone else, to my children or anyone else. But ultimately–in this case–it doesn't matter to me."

Was she planning to file a lawsuit? "Lots of attorneys have contacted me," she says with a grim, tight little smile. From a relative in the banking business she learned of compensation formulas. "He told me how to calculate a person's worth." Her voice is faint, distant. "I know something about that. Delta has contacted me. Delta's insurance companies have contacted me." Seven weeks after the crash, they had yet to make a monetary offer, asking only for facts about the family. "People keep saying, 'Oh, you have to have an attorney.' But I don't think I can be manipulated. Maybe I'm wrong. I mean, they talk about it so mysteriously."

32   Part of her simply doesn't want to prolong the anguish, and part of her doesn't even want the money. "Even insurance money–which is something you pay for, something you buy–is upsetting to me. I realize it's just to support the children. But"–for an instant there is a cold fire in those soft eyes–"if anybody suggests that they are paying me for my grief, that's just ludicrous."

Where does she go from here? "I don't know. Actually, I think I'm one of those people who is very good at blocking out things they don't want to feel. I think I'll be seeing a psychiatrist for quite a while."

In the weeks just after the crash, Leora spent a lot of time watching Ron and

Annie on video tapes, electronic snatches of life freeze-framed, rewound, and played again in a darkened room. Images of times past, of laughter, and a life cut short. Images of Ron with his beard, the one he shaved off so the age-guesser at Six Flags would lop half a dozen years off his life.

Perhaps Dana is too young to remember the feel of her father's soft brown whiskers against her baby-soft skin. But not Annie. She took it hard. When Leora told her that her father was dead, she cried, "That's not fair!" The second thing she said was, "I'm not going to have any more brothers and sisters." The Whites were planning for another child. Why not? The first fruits of ten and a half years of hard work were just being twisted from the tree. Two hours after the shock, Annie sat down in front of the television and said, "I'm not going to think about it any more. I'm not going to be sad." This worried Leora: "I'm not sure that's the healthiest way to deal with it. She has to deal with it."

Thus, Annie's airplane. After talking with the psychiatrist, Leora took her daughter to a toy shop. "I didn't try to put it in her head," says Leora. "We were just there and I said, 'Look, here's an airplane.'" When she saw it, the child replied, "Oh boy! I bet Papa would like to play with that."

TRAUMA

At 18:06, within seconds of the crash, Department of Public Safety radios across DFW crackled to life: "Report of heavy jet crash at north end of airport." The notification sparked a massive rescue effort. Although the response wasn't textbook, it undeniably saved lives, lots of lives.

A DFW Mobile Intensive Care Unit was the first medical help to arrive on the scene. It was there within two minutes. Immediately, paramedics saw that they needed help. They called for medical trailers and supplies to be sent to the east air freight area. Then they began triage.

The word is from the French. It means, literally, "to sort." Under the battlefield-tested theory of triage, there are three categories of casualties—not human beings, but casualties. In triage, cold logic, not necessarily compassion, is the governing principle. The theory assumes few caregivers and many in need of care. Triage demarks the quick from the dead. There are those who will probably die regardless of the care administered, those who will likely live, and those on the cusp. It is to the latter that first, best efforts are directed. Clear their airway, stop their bleeding, treat them for shock, and transport them to a hospital first. Then they have a decent chance.

By 18:18, DFW paramedics had established a triage area and medical command post near the tail of the TriStar. Urgent calls for more help had been broadcast. But for the first critical few minutes, DFW paramedics were on their own. It is estimated that at least 50 percent of those treated at the triage site wouldn't have made it without them.

The first outside help came from ambulances dispatched by nearby Hurst-Euless-Bedford Hospital and a private ambulance company. They arrived at 18:27. The first helicopter was overhead three minutes later. Within the next half hour, a small army arrived. Jack Ayers was one of the shock troops.

At first glance, the thirty-eight-year-old native Texan seems an unlikely foot soldier. He is one of the most successful attorneys in Dallas. His clothes, office, and demeanor speak more of boardrooms and Bally shoes than accident scenes and hip boots. Appearances bely his background as former commander of the suburban Richardson Police Department's crack Special Operations Division. While he was with the department, he realized that he was "functionally incompetent to take care of people [medically] in the field." And so he became a paramedic.

His internship was with the Dallas Fire Department in sometimes-volatile South Dallas. Residency was at Parkland Hospital, the area's premier trauma center.

Eventually Ayers combined his legal vocation and medical avocation to become a teacher at the University of Texas Health Science Center at Dallas. His specialty was the legal aspects of emergency medical services. It was virgin territory, especially the critical question of patient consent.

During the administration of President Carter, the young attorney became the chief legal adviser on EMS legal issues in the United States. So impressed was the Department of Transportation with his work that they asked him to write the standard text on the subject.

It had been the end of a long week. Ayers was working late at his far–North Dallas office. As volunteer head of Parkland's Emergency Legal Assistance Program, he was on call. Sometime after 6:15, the phone rang. Was the hospital's disaster plan operable? Before he could ask why, his office manager came in. There had been a crash. It was serious.

He got in his car and headed toward LBJ Freeway, all the while monitoring the police radio. In lawyerly fashion he says, "I felt it was prudent for me to get moving south [towards Parkland]." He heard that paramedic units in Northwest and West Dallas were being dispatched to DFW. As he merged onto crowded I-635, it soon became obvious that "they were screaming for ambulances." Rather than going to Parkland, Jack Ayers raced for DFW.

Tucking in behind a rescue vehicle and pulling up to the east cargo area just before 6:45, he was in luck. The officer guarding the entrance was one of Ayers's former pupils. Within minutes, he was at the triage area. By then, there were some fifteen ambulances on the scene, "but they were all of the basic life support level. There weren't, that I could see, that many paramedics. That was the problem. Because when I got there, my estimate was that there were probably ten or fifteen patients, maybe twenty, that I could identify as being alive."

One of them lay on his back, a victim of "massive crushing distortion, massive internal injuries." And yet he still agonizingly gasped for breath. "If it was simply a single car accident, you would give them treatment," he sighs, covering his face with his hands as the memories flood in. "But there weren't enough facilities, nor enough time."

"The one [patient] I guess I remember the best is the guy who kept asking me if he was dead. It sounds like a silly question, but he was sincere. He really wondered if he'd survived. He was burned and sitting on the steps of a vehicle. I had him lie down and started an IV on him."

In response to the man's understandable, if macabre, question, Ayers gently told him to lie down, get his feet up so he could breathe. Compliantly, he did as he was asked. "I don't think he survived," says Ayers.

After seeing eight to ten patients, none of whom he believes made it, Ayers donned hip boots and, with a paramedic he knew, waded into hell. "We went up to the front part of the fuselage where there were large balls of material, up by the water tower. There were large balls of metal and seats and things. We had a common fear: that there was someone alive in there who was trapped."

Together, the pair slogged through the muck left when the water tower ruptured. Acrid ash assaulted their nostrils. Thick, black mire pulled at their legs like a living entity, threatening to swallow them whole, drag them body and soul into the pit of unspeakable pity ploughed by the disintegrating fuselage.

"We went through there and determined pretty quickly that everybody was dead. Many of the bodies were so badly dismembered and burned that it was obvious. From everything I saw, the destruction [of the aircraft] at that point was complete. A lot of the bodies were still strapped in their seats. Maybe you would find two or three piled on top of one another, like they had come out in rows almost, just stacked on top of one another and buried in that mud. It was the damnedest thing that I ever saw." Still, for all the utter destruction, Ayers and his companion wanted to make sure there wasn't "an air pocket where somebody could have survived." For half an hour or forty-five minutes they looked. They found nothing.

After another futile check of the triage area, the lawyer took hold. Jack Ayers started to compile a list of survivors for transmission to Parkland. By this time, hospital switchboards in the area were swamped with calls from frantic relatives, each wanting to know if their husband, their mother, their son was alive. If the fates wouldn't allow him the role of healer, at least he could comfort.

While he was compiling the list, a DFW Department of Public Safety official told Ayers that he was concerned about the serrated aluminum skin of the L10. **37** Rescue workers were being cut out there, and he was afraid of tetanus. Ayers and another paramedic left for Parkland to pick up a supply of vaccine and syringes. While there, he would also cross-check the list of survivors.

When Jack Ayers walked in the emergency room, it was as if a spectre had entered. Still decked out in hip boots and bloody shirt, he was like a leper. "They didn't say anything. It just got quiet. Dead quiet." The frenetic activity of the emergency room stopped cold. The people assembled at Parkland were optimists. They hoped, felt, knew that *their* loved one was among the living. "Those people didn't want to talk to me," remembers Ayers. "They didn't want to be disabused of that notion." The foul-smelling, muck-caked paramedic was a walking reminder of the carnage of 191, a grim visage whose presence was more evocative of death than media reports could ever hope to be.

As Ayers disappeared to gather supplies, there was a collective exhalation. The strange, arrhythmic pulse of the place resumed.

Parkland, the designated trauma center for the area, first got word to expect anywhere from twenty to fifty critically burned patients. Patients started to arrive by helicopter around 18:35, even before the hospital's triage team, consisting of two surgeons and two nurses, could arrive on the scene. "The first one in," recalls Beth Mancini, Parkland's director of emergency services, "was an 80 percent burn. Male. All third degree. He went directly to the burn unit."

On the same flight was a teenager with fractures and minor burns on the extremities. Next to arrive was an ambulance with five walking wounded. The Steinbergs were among them.

Waiting to meet the expected deluge in the emergency room were fifty physicians and at least an equal number of nurses. The crash had occurred at a "good" time. People were either still at work, on their way home, or in front of their television sets watching the news when word of 191 was first broadcast. The response was virtually automatic. Parkland is the teaching hospital for the adjoining University of Texas Health Science Center at Dallas. In the Department of Surgery, staffers, teachers, and residents dropped what they were doing and headed for the ER. Activation of the department's disaster plan was a moot exercise; people had assumed it was in effect the moment they heard the news.

Between 18:35 and 19:00, the tempo of the ER crescendoed. At one point, the trickle seemed to become a tidal wave. The notion was compounded by relatives, curiosity seekers, and members of the press who began to strain against security personnel. "We could have handled 200 survivors," maintains Mancini. Indeed, on an average day, Parkland's emergency room treats some 450 patients.

As the injured arrived by ambulance and air, a remarkable phenomenon was forming just across Harry Hines Boulevard, the broad thoroughfare that fronts the gargantuan medical complex. It was a line of people. As twilight became night, it swelled. Yet it was orderly, almost somber. These were neither curiosity seekers nor death junkies. They were life-givers. They too had heard of the crash on their way home. And they were there to offer the only thing they could: their blood. Parkland public relations chief Greg Graze remembers being asked by a Channel 8 reporter, " 'Shall we put out an appeal for blood?' I thought for a couple of seconds," remembers Graze, "and said, 'Yeah, I think we're going to need it.' " Between 18:30 Friday night and 2:30 the following morning, more than 1,300 people turned out. "We ended up

38

drawing 764 units," says Graze. "We just couldn't accommodate all the people who wanted to give."

Flight 191 had galvanized the city of Dallas like no event since the assassination of John F. Kennedy. Ironically, the physical focus was the same as before: the nondescript emergency entrance of the city's charity hospital. But there was a difference: almost twenty-two years earlier, all Dallasites could do was wring their hands in abject frustration, perhaps join in collective prayer. Now, *this* time, they could do something. "This was our hometown," says former journalist Graze. "Our great, wonderful airport where it could never possibly happen. These were people just like us. And here their lives were completely disrupted, changed forever. In some cases, whole families were wiped out. It just had a tremendous impact. It left an indelible imprint."

As the stream of blood donors swelled to a river, the flow of patients abruptly stopped. "There was this little thing that happened around seven o'clock," remembers Beth Mancini, in a choked, unnaturally husky whisper. "Part of you was saying, 'Oh, my God! Will they ever stop coming in?' You're hoping you can do the very best for everybody and organize everything. Suddenly, there's nobody else. It became very quiet. We just knew when that last [triage] team came in—that's it."

The last patient to arrive at Parkland directly from the scene was Baby X. The infant was found lying among pieces of the aluminum pyre by a priest. The child's injuries were obvious: virtually every square inch of its body was burned. And yet it breathed.

Tenderly, the child was lifted from the helicopter and carried to the ER. Efforts at resuscitation failed. "The baby was very hard to take," says Beth Mancini. "I mean, I've held a lot of dead and dying babies, and that hurt. He had these tiny little sandals. That thought will stay with me a long time."

Fire exacted a heavy toll. Of the twenty-one patients admitted to Parkland on August 2, seven suffered from significant burns. A third-degree burn is the most profound insult the human body can suffer. The body's prime shield against infection, the skin, is destroyed. Yet infection, while it often proves to be the ultimate killer, is not the immediate threat. Pam Walter is a head nurse on Burn Unit Six North. She speaks concisely, clinically—verbal evidence of the psychic armor she must don each day to handle one of the most emotionally draining jobs in medicine: "Initially, when a patient is burned, rather than being so concerned with the depth of the burn, it's the extent of the burn, what we call the percentage of the body burned. There are several reasons for that. If the patient has any sort of significant burn whatsoever, when you're burned, you lose fluid through that burn. Your skin, normally being intact, holds fluid inside your body. When you remove skin through a burn, the fluid oozes out. If you have a large enough percentage of the body burned, then you can

39

lose tremendous amounts of fluid. If that were untreated, a person would go into shock because he had become so dehydrated. The blood pressure would drop," due to the huge fluid loss.

The first step in treating a burn victim, aside from ensuring that the patient can breathe, is to estimate the percentage of burn. At the same time, IVs of Ringers Lactate (an isotonic solution that most nearly resembles the body's natural fluids) are started. If you can get a severely burned patient through the first twenty-four hours, the chance of shock diminishes greatly.

The formula for life is precise: In the case of an adult male of 150 pounds burned over 80 percent of his body, multiply his weight in kilograms (approximately half the weight in pounds, or in this instance 75) times the percentage of burn. Then, this figure is multiplied times a known amount of replacement fluid, in this case 4 cc of Ringers. "That averages out to 240,000 cc," says Walter. "If you're talking about a liter of fluid, it's 24." Twenty-four liters for 24 hours. Life-giving liters. So critical is the body's need for moisture that the stuff is often fed via two or three IVs fitted directly into any remaining large veins.

The popular notion is that a profoundly burned person feels no pain. "That's true, technically," says Walter. "With a third-degree burn, you've damaged the skin deeply enough that the nerve endings are destroyed. But the thing to remember is that in a second-degree burn, the nerve endings are still intact. And a burn wound is very rarely all second or all third. It's more commonly a mixture of different degrees."

On admission to the unit, after their breathing and fluid levels have been stabilized, victims are bathed. The process is essential, yet the pain can be excruciating. Raw nerve endings are exposed to unwanted stimulation. Washing removes "any debris, blisters, or dead skin that may be covering new skin. All that dead tissue is a source of infection." And infection is "inevitable." The idea is to stave it off, limit its virulence. Silvadene helps. It's a cool, white substance the consistency of cold cream. The broad spectrum antibiotic is applied to massive burns three times a day. In Parkland's burn units, it often takes the place of dressings.

The unit is strict about sterility. Visitors scrub, gown, and mask before finally **40** donning surgical gloves. The staff members gown when they leave the unit so they won't take germs with them.

When infection comes, it's often in the form of *Pseudomonas*, a gram-negative organism that can mutate just often enough to keep one step ahead of any effective counter. "How rapidly it moves will depend on where you initially find it," says Walter. There are a host of potential invasion sites. Most common is the burn wound itself, followed by the lungs and IV and catheter insertions.

A change in skin color is one of the first signs of the potential killer. The tinge at first is yellowish, later brown or black as any remaining healthy skin is invaded. Another cream, Sulfamyalon, is thrown into the battle. If the strain of *Pseudomonas* isn't too exotic, if the antibiotic is right, the patient can hang on while skin grafts have a chance to replace the body's natural barrier.

Victims of plane crashes often succumb to something called ARDS, Adult Respiratory Distress Syndrome. The lungs too are burned, seared by the inhalation of superhot gasses or, more likely, chemical reactions from burning plastics. Normally healthy pink lung tissue itself becomes an open wound.

Five of the seven significantly burned patients admitted to Parkland made it to burn units. Baby X died in the ER. Of those five, four died as a result of their burns. One fought off infection only to face another ordeal. The seventh person, never admitted to a burn unit, was discharged.

In all, thirty-one people from Flight 191 were treated that evening at area hospitals, twenty-one of them at Parkland—twenty-one people in a place geared to handle ten times that many. "Actually, it was a relatively quiet Friday night [in terms of sheer numbers]," muses Beth Mancini. "But there was something about the fact you knew that the other 130 were dead. There was this terrible sense of—" She knots her fists. "When you go into this field, the doctors, the nurses, the people who work at Parkland are here because they want to help people. You're all here. You're ready. You have some twenty-odd rooms prepared to take critically burned people. You're standing here with the very best, the most technically sophisticated equipment. And suddenly, there's nobody here that needs your help. It's not frustrating," she says softly. "It's sad."

The human toll of August 2 wasn't confined to victims and families. Rescuers and care-givers too were affected. Pat Bechtel-Mehling is the ER's chaplain. In the weeks following the crash, she counseled those who worked that night. "People still come in," she says, "and discuss their dreams. They have dreams of airplane crashes. Things falling out of the sky. Death. Lots of death."

Those who work in emergency medicine are faint of neither heart nor hand. They develop defense mechanisms to keep death at bay. Rationality is the order of the day, tempered by measured doses of compassion. For many, 191 shattered that shield, left it scattered like shards of serrated aluminum. "A lot of things happen here [at the ER] that we can justify—either rightly or wrongly," says Bechtel-Mehling. "They shouldn't have been at that bar. They shouldn't have been out there by themselves at night. All those kinds of things. This, you can't. I mean, there's no way we can escape the fact that this can happen to us. It becomes personal and we do all kinds of things to keep death from being personal to us."

One ninety-one became personal to a lot of people, among them a guy named Bob Sonnamaker.

41

RING OF LIGHT

Each October, a portion of old East
Dallas becomes one of the great showplaces on earth, home of hucksters, hustlers,
and homefolk. The Texas State Fair is the biggest production of its kind, an extrava-
ganza presided over by the larger-than-life visage of Big Tex. The towering giant in
the ten-gallon hat has boomed out hearty "Howdys!" to generations of fairgoers.
Before *Dallas* became Friday-night fare across the nation, before downtown became
a gaucherie of glazed glass, even before Roger Staubach, Big Tex was Big D.

The man behind the monster mannequin is an unassuming native Texan of
middle age and average height. While his voice gives the giant speech, his hands
bequeath something more basic: life itself.

Bob Sonnamaker is an emergency medical technician by avocation and a
professional audio engineer by profession. The free-lance sound man has worked on
movie sets, at fairs and has even owned a recording studio. "The Rolling Stones were
never one of my clients," he chuckles.

"Working on movie sets can be a very dangerous business," he adds.
"Things are not always as they appear. A person can lean against a wall—it *looks* like
a wall—and really it's a piece of canvas held up by a board." Accidents happen, some
of them serious. Sonnamaker became a sort of unofficial medic for the crews, a guy
who could treat a burn from a klieg light or splint a broken ankle. Dabbling became
diligence. As long as people were going to come to him for help anyway, he figured
he might as well learn to do it right. And so he became an EMT.

In the more than one hundred hours it took him to earn his license,
Sonnamaker learned how to bandage, administer CPR, insert an airway, attach a
cervical collar, and perform other lifesaving techniques. The instruction didn't come
cheap, nor did the well-stocked trauma kit he always carries in the trunk of his car.
No one pays Bob Sonnamaker to help people. He does it because he wants to. "I
honestly believe it's a need, not only in me, but in everyone. Maybe there's a little

43

ego thing, too. I'm not a believer in Eastern religions, but my understanding of Karma
is that if you do nice things for other people, nice things are going to happen to you."
There's little pretense to the man, much that is persuasive. His car is unadorned by
boast or bumper sticker. The only thing that differentiates it from others on the street
is the small EMT emblem on the windshield.

Sonnamaker earned his license in late May 1985. He expected that he might
have to use his skills someday to save a life. But he never guessed that "someday"
would come so soon.

On Friday, August 2, Sonnamaker decided he would water the lawn of his
home in near–North Dallas. "It was really a typical hot Texas day. There was the possibility of showers, but I always go ahead and water anyway because the possibility of
showers means a 1 percent chance at my house." That afternoon a friend called. She
needed a ride to DFW. Her flight to San Francisco was at seven. Could she leave her
car at Bob's house and make it to the airport in time for a drink before boarding?

Friday afternoon rush hour can be a gridlock in the burgeoning metroplex
of Dallas–Fort Worth, especially in the mid-cities area near the airport. Bob's friend
usually took Texas Highway 114 to DFW. It was a straight shot from Northwest Dallas.
Since Bob was driving, he recommended another route: "Have you ever taken the LBJ
Freeway? It might be a bit longer, but it's faster. No lights." As it turned out, taking
the Lyndon Baines Johnson Freeway did save a few minutes. It may also have saved
their lives.

As they headed west toward the airport, before their eyes a monstrous cloud
blossomed north of the field like some mutant purple wildflower. In addition to being
an EMT, Sonnamaker is a ham radio operator and trained weather observer. He says
he saw a "big cumulonimbus" formation. "I really couldn't see the top of it. I could
see a lot of rain, a lot of lightning." He describes the leading edge of the storm as
a "wall of rain." His main concern was to make it to the terminal before the thing hit.
He didn't. The cars that didn't pull to the side of the road slowed to a virtual crawl.

He made a sweeping left-hand arc to the south, across the overpass leading
to the long central drive that bisects the world's second-largest airport. It was still raining when he pulled into a sheltered underground departure area and dropped his
friend off. Just as he pulled out and headed north again, the local all-news radio station, KRLD, broke in with a bulletin: there was an unconfirmed report that a plane
had gone down at DFW.

Sonnamaker spotted the flames almost immediately. He exited the turnstile
plaza and bore right along a service road towards the east air freight area. On the way
over, he had time to think. His breathing quickened, his triphammer heart providing
visceral counterpoint to the radio reports that were just starting to come in. "I can't
describe my feelings at that time. It was scary."

Within minutes of the crash, he was on the scene. Police hadn't yet had a chance to set up a crowd-control perimeter. Pulling up outside a fence that had apparently been flattened by the plane, Sonnamaker grabbed his orange trauma kit, vaulted over the jumbled barrier, and found himself struggling through a mire of thick, black mud. Twice, the suction of the stuff pulled off his shoes. The morass was the product not so much of the rain as rich, deep soil and seven million gallons of water from the ruptured tank.

Sonnamaker was confronted by the smoldering, jumbled entrails of the eviscerated aluminum creature. "I didn't see anything that looked remotely like an airplane except for the tail section. Nothing else made any sense at all." Save for the tail and a scattering of seats, "everything was just tiny pieces—nuts and bolts and things that looked like camshafts—wiring and pieces, just tiny pieces."

And then there were the people. "It was like looking at mannequins. It was as if a department store had taken all their old, broken, disfigured, and discarded mannequins—some clothed, some not clothed, some with torn clothing—and put them in a rubbish heap or the back of a big dump truck." In his EMT training at Dallas's Baylor Hospital, "they showed me some pretty gruesome visuals. I'm glad they did. It prepared me to be not quite as"—his voice falls to a hoarse whisper—"aghast."

Remember the television spot where the sad-eyed kid slowly, imperceptibly looks up at the screen? Click, click, click. The child looks up. It's as if time has taken on another reality—heightened, almost suspended. There is only the moment. And the moment is forever. The late afternoon of August 2 was like that for the novice EMT. "It was like a slide show without the dissolves. Quick cuts." Click, click, click. "I'm a student of film, and one of Fellini's techniques is to put people in situations they don't want to be in. Hypothetically, he might open the scene with a very tight shot of a barrel of dead fish. There you are with a full screen of dead fish, and you don't want to be there. It was a place I did not want to be."

Disregarding the tail section a few hundred yards away, Sonnamaker concentrated on the middle section of what had been the fuselage. North, towards Highway 114 and the water tanks, nothing lived. South, in the tail, there were signs of movement. Here, in the middle, life might, just might, still hang by a thread. "Seeing all those seats and people, I started a zigzag motion back and forth across the area, trying to find *somebody* alive." In freeze-frame he moved, the sound of sirens muted by light rain, rain that draped the dead like a shroud of dirty gauze.

Most of the mannequins were obviously dead, trauma so severe as to be "incompatible with life." With others, he felt for a pulse. He was halfway through the middle section of seats and still found nothing but utter desolation. Sonnamaker had been on the scene for thirty minutes. The storm that had come out of nowhere, passed just as quickly. From the west, rays of the dying sun filtered through the trailing

45

tendrils of the beast, casting shafts of shadow and light. One of these shafts reflected off a piece of metal. Unlike the dirty grey patina of the surrounding aluminum, this one glinted gold. And it moved.

The ring was extraordinary – patterned and very pretty: a wedding ring. The hand to which it was attached was faintly warm, reddened by the flash fire that had swept the cabin. Through the wrist, blood pulsed – weakly, to be sure, but surely nonetheless. It was the first sign of life Sonnamaker had seen in an eternity.

As if startled from a daze, he stood up and yelled for help. He needed assistance in removing the row of three seats that lay atop the passenger. Before lifting the seats, Sonnamaker used his trauma scissors to cut the seat belt. Gently, the other rescuers who had arrived lifted the assembly. Underneath was a woman. "Her head was in an unnatural position," remembers Sonnamaker. "Her jacket, like a pants suit jacket, was pulled up over her face from the back covering her face." Carefully, he cut it away. The strange position of her head seemed to scream spinal injury, and he didn't want to make things worse. He made sure she was breathing, then attached a surgical collar to prevent further injury. A paramedic arrived and inserted an oral pharangeal airway. She was delicately placed on a backboard for evacuation.

As she was taken away, Bob Sonnamaker wondered who the woman was. He had gotten a hint when he cut away the jacket. Stitched into the collar was a laundry label. On it was a name: Ford.

A month earlier, thirty-five-year-old Kathy Ford had come home to Fort Worth to begin a new assignment with Delphi, a business computer firm. Although happy with their work, she and her husband Terry – a Delphi vice president – didn't like the company's Southern California base. Texas was the place they wanted to be. Terry resigned; Kathy tried to. Delphi's reaction to the prospect of losing perhaps the company's most productive manager was immediate: they created a job for her, in Texas.

Kathy Ford, wife, corporate executive, mother of two, and gourmet cook, is the kind of person you see profiled in women's magazines. She's a cheerleader without artifice, an achiever without affectation.

46

Terry and Kathy had met four years earlier. He was western division manager for Reynolds and Reynolds, another computer company. She was a would-be salesperson. When the regional manager for Texas recommended that Kathy be hired on the sales staff, Ford – a hard-driving, no-nonsense type with traditional values – didn't like the idea. "I didn't think that she should be hired as a salesman," recalls Terry, "because I didn't think that women did that great a job. My regional manager hung right in there and kept trying to hire her. I said, 'Hey, you do what you want to do. The burden's on you, though. I'm going to make you responsible.' "

The decision changed his perception of women. It also changed his life. Within half a year, Kathy was in the top 5 percent of the sales force. Ford was impressed, so much so that he went out on a limb to get her admitted to the company's exclusive 300 Club, an elite group of sales achievers. "I virtually put my career on the line. I said, 'Look, I know it's against our rules to send a person who doesn't have a full year [on the job], but *this* person–' We got her in."

Ford was impressed by more than her productivity. She was vivacious, attractive, and *simpatica.* They fell in love. By 1982, the pieces had all fallen in place for Terry. After seventeen years with Reynolds and Reynolds, he was at the pinnacle of his profession. Now was the time for Terry and Kathy to spread their wings, personally and professionally. They married, quit the company, and set out for Abilene to start their own business. The young couple arrived in West Texas just in time to fall victim to the collapse of the domestic petroleum market. Their move had been partially predicated on the heady rise in oil prices and the industry's need for tools to manage the exponential growth. "We sold out before we went down with the business," says Terry. They returned to California, their dream of independence on hold.

The summer of 1985 found them back in Texas, Kathy with the challenging assignment of breaking ground for a sales force in the southeast and Terry back in the executive suite with another computer firm. Kathy's children by an earlier marriage, thirteen-year-old Jody and seventeen-year-old Jamie, were getting ready to enter school. Texas was their home, and that meant buying a house. They found the perfect place in the Saddlebrook subdivision of suburban Fort Worth: "semi-Texas, semi-California, all glass," smiles Terry. "We'd spaced out a pool in the backyard." The home fit into their plans of eventually striking out on their own again. They wanted to get an accelerated payment schedule, pay it off within a few years, and semiretire while they were still relatively young. When she took off on a routine business trip to South Florida on Wednesday, July 31, Kathy had already begun to decorate the home in her mind. They had planned to make an offer on the place on Saturday, August 3, after she got back.

Until they got settled in, Terry, Kathy, and the kids were staying with a relative. Kathy's family had their roots in Fort Worth. In the hot, hazy week in which July melted into August, Terry was traveling on business. Spontaneity was very much a part of their relationship. He decided to come home on Thursday, August 1, and surprise her when she arrived that evening from Fort Lauderdale. Thinking Terry wouldn't be home until Friday, Kathy decided to stay over and help a salesperson with a client. She would catch a Delta flight to DFW the following afternoon. As frequent flyers, both she and Terry made it a point to fly the airline whenever they could. They liked the service and the attitude. It was a lot like their own: assertive with a human touch.

FIRE & RAIN

On Friday afternoon, Terry had just returned from the cleaners, where he had picked up some clothes for his next trip. He would be hitting the road Saturday afternoon, just as soon as they had made the offer on the house. As he walked in, the relative with whom they were staying looked up from the couch with a somber look on her face. She had been watching TV. The announcer had said there had been a crash at DFW. "Fear strikes you," says Terry softly. "Yet you say, 'Well, how many planes come in on Friday night?' " He already knew the answer: lots. Still, he checked with Delta. When he asked the person on the other end of the line if the plane from Fort Lauderdale had arrived, there was a pause: "Hold on just a second." "The absolute fear of God struck me," he shivers. After a long wait, the agent was on the line again: "Ah, who are you again? What did you want?" His wife was on a flight from Fort Lauderdale. It was supposed to arrive about 5:30 or 6:00. Was it in yet? "Hold on. Let me check another time."

"It's not possible!" his mind screamed. In a minute, the agent was back on: "We don't show anything. But the plane is supposed to arrive tonight." "I *knew* that was wrong," says Terry emphatically. "I'd been flying for too many years. I knew she was snowballing me, because they'll tell you exactly whether the plane's late, whether it's late taking off, that it's anticipated being in, that it's in. But they're not going to be vague and say, 'Well, yeah, there's a flight coming in, but who knows when.' " It was impractical not to believe that Kathy's flight had crashed. Still, he didn't want to believe it. Hanging up the phone, he went back to listen to the news reports. The plane was a Delta L1011, Flight 191 from Fort Lauderdale. "My life absolutely stopped."

He ran to the bedroom he was sharing with Kathy, fumbled for his attache case, and pulled out a map of Dallas. He wasn't familiar with the town. As he sprinted toward his car, Jamie followed. Terry wanted the boy to stay with the relative because of her age, "But I couldn't ask him to do that. It was his mother." The first stop was the mid-cities Hurst-Euless-Bedford Hospital. He had heard that some of the survivors had been initially taken there. Kathy wasn't among them. Terry called Parkland. They wouldn't release any information on the phone.

Terry and Jamie arrived in front of Parkland about seven o'clock. Traffic was heavy, exacerbated by the two-block line of people, three and four abreast, who had gathered along Dallas's busy Harry Hines Boulevard to donate blood. Parking the car, the pair ran toward the emergency room entrance. "Police attempted to stop us," says Ford. "I told them there was no way."

At the desk, he identified himself. Quickly, he learned that a woman had been admitted who hadn't been positively identified. They thought they knew who she was but couldn't be sure. Terry identified his petite, pretty wife in detail. A nurse left for a moment. When she returned, there was a business card in her hand. "It was burned, almost gone, with the exception of Kathy's name and Delphi." The nurse hadn't wanted to show him the blackened piece of cardboard, but it was the only way to be sure.

Kathy was alive. Strangely, it didn't surprise him. He had expected it. There is a force of will about Ford, evidenced by his commanding baritone voice, his carriage, and his track record. On his dash to Dallas, he virtually willed that his wife be among the living. "I knew she was there. I knew she was there all the way over on Highway 183. I was talking to God all the way and I knew she was here [at Parkland]. I didn't know how bad she was, didn't know what the situation was. But I knew she was here. It wasn't me. It was the Good Lord letting me know he hadn't taken her."

Kathy Ford was the third or fourth person to arrive at Parkland from the crash scene. She was preceded by a sixteen-year-old boy and a man with massive burns. Dr. Dan Myer, a third-year resident from Los Angeles, was the first physician to treat her. He was on his way home when he heard the page for chief residents to call the ER. "I happened to be on the service with one of them, so I knew I wouldn't be leaving." Word began to circulate that there had been a plane crash. Parkland holds drills intermittently, so most people didn't know whether it was rumor or reality. They soon found out.

When Kathy was rolled into one of the trauma rooms, "she was not moving around," says Myer. "She already had an airway established. She had obvious abdominal distension and deep second-degree burns on her hands and legs. She was in a C [cervical] collar. The really significant thing was that her blood pressure was low. She wasn't breathing on her own and was very shocky." Had she remained buried under those seats (she was in 30C) for much more than a half hour, she probably wouldn't have made it to Parkland. Bob Sonnamaker, beckoned by a beam of light, had saved her life.

After checking respiration and heart rate, Myer increased the flow from the IV that had already been inserted. It was imperative that he raise her blood pressure, save her from the killing shadow of shock. The young resident then made a quick evaluation of the other apparent injuries. "She had this obvious intercranial injury. We weren't sure where at that point. The lungs were clear. We really couldn't tell anything from our abdominal exam because she wasn't responding." The best way to determine internal bleeding is to insert a needle into the abdomen just through the skin to see if there is any blood. If the syringe comes up red, that means an emergency operation. "I obtained blood out of one side, but not the other. That means it's hard to interpret. So we did what's called a diagnostic peritoneal lavage, where we make a small incision in the abdomen and run one liter of IV fluid in. Then, in a cycle effect, we take it back out and analyze it to see if she needs an operation." A breakdown of the number of white and red blood cells is performed. "Chemical analyses and studies have been

49

done to show if people with certain numbers of red blood cells have true abdominal injuries," says Myer.

Kathy's exam was inconclusive. Myer says that she had apparently once had at least one small operation. This hampered the lavage: "You can't move the fluid around and it gets stuck in little pockets." They'd have to do exploratory surgery. But before that, there was the equally pressing matter of her head injury. Before the skull could be opened up, doctors needed a road map. A sophisticated Computerized Axial Tomography, or CAT scan, would show them where the damage was. It's a technique of advanced X-ray photography that produces a three-dimensional picture of a portion of the human body. In this case, the images it produced were sobering.

After treating the woman he had rescued from beneath the seats, Bob Sonnamaker retraced his steps at a faster pace. One last look, just to be sure. Then he headed for his car. On the way out, he drove past the triage area to see if he could be of any help there. "By this time, there were fifty ambulances there. I turned around and left. The media was just arriving. I was leaving. I was through."

He has no memory of the drive home. Lights, traffic, the incessant buzz of further bulletins about the crash on the car radio—nothing registered. When he arrived home, a friend was waiting. "It would have been very bad, I think, if that person hadn't been. I understand now that the people who have the most problem with post-traumatic stress syndrome are the people who are not able to talk it out. They keep it all in." Inside the haven of his own home, Sonnamaker began to talk. "My clothes were dirty. I was muddy, bloody, smelling of burned flesh. The smell was still on my clothes. I offered a brief explanation, put my clothes in the washer, and took a shower." As the hot spray washed away the day's death, the slide show flickered on the inside of his eyelids. Later, he poured a double shot of Jack Daniels and sat down in front of the television to watch the rest of the story.

Around eight o'clock that night, the rest of the family got the word that Kathy was alive. By 9:15 they had arrived at Parkland. There are four sisters in the family. One of them is Carol Christy, an attractive thirty-four-year-old who works in Fort Worth's court system.

When the family arrived, a staff member met them at the door of the ER. "Whoever met us there knew. They could just tell [we were family]. The security guards took us up to the cafeteria area. That's where everyone was. They ushered us into the room and we gathered around a large table. Kathy was in surgery and one of the chaplains went up to get Terry."

The main-floor cafeteria was haven amidst holocaust. As the interminable evening wore on, some 150 people gathered in the family-only enclave. "From what

I understand," says Carol, "we were the only family in the room that had a survivor." Delta and Parkland provisioned the cafeteria with food, blankets, and pillows. Guards flanked the doors, attempting to make sure that the prayers, the grieving of those within, were private things.

While awaiting word on her operation, Kathy's family gathered around a table for one of the score of impromptu prayer services that filled the room that evening. As they prayed out their innermost hopes and fears, someone other than The Almighty was listening.

On Saturday morning, after a night of fuzzed semisleep, Carol Christy began to read about 191. One of the stories in the *Dallas Morning News* told of a woman in a red jumpsuit, the same ensemble Carol was wearing. Still a bit groggy from the ordeal, Carol read on. Strange. Then, the piece mentioned the family of Carol Ford. "This is *us*," she gasped. "They're talking about us!" The *Morning News* then replayed in print the family's prayers of the night before. According to Carol, the family never talked to the reporter, never even knew he was there. "Very obviously, there was someone very near to us in the room. We were far enough away from the door so that someone had to be in there listening. I was very offended. It was a terrible invasion of our privacy. We certainly wouldn't have talked to a reporter at that time."

After some seven hours of surgery to repair abdominal injuries caused by the seat belt, Kathy was wheeled to intensive care. The abdominal injuries, the burns, and a fractured ankle would heal, the family was told. But not her head.

On Friday afternoon, at almost precisely 6:05:58, the occupants of the first three-fourths of the cabin of Flight 191 had been subject to massive deceleration. Newton's third law of motion played havoc on human bodies. People became rag dolls as limbs snapped, internal organs exploded, and spines whipsawed. Kathy Ford was more fortunate than most. She survived in a section of the TriStar where most life ceased in a microsecond. But she paid for it. On impact, the lower part of her brain, the brain stem, sheared. After being stabilized and taken to ICU, a special tube was inserted into her skull to measure intercranial pressure. "They didn't do any procedure on the brain," says Dr. Dan Myer. Was there none to be done? Myer answers almost inaudibly: "Unfortunately."

51

Twelve weeks after the accident, Terry Ford sits in a Wendy's a couple of blocks from Parkland. Kathy has been out of intensive care for two weeks. Dressed in jeans, a western shirt, and boots, he looks tired. His voice doesn't betray it: "From the first day till today—as often as it seems they get the chance—they've given me a definite negative prognosis." He leans back in the chair and takes a sip of a Pepsi, his "dinner." In fact, Kathy will virtually not be any different from a neurological point of view than she is right now. But then, what does that really mean? She is, he explains, "dramatically different" twelve weeks after the accident.

When he first saw her in surgical intensive care, she was "lying there in an absolutely lifeless form." Until she was transferred to a regular room, the family only got to see her four times a day for periods of ten minutes per visit. At best, Terry could only take mental snapshots of her progress, momentary pictures projected against a backdrop of hope. "When you see her four times a day for ten minutes, you don't get a good look at the whole situation. Some of the things I thought might have been responsiveness when she was in intensive care—because she was doing them while I was in there—I've come to find out may be things she's doing all the time," things like certain movements, expressions.

Because of that, doctors deemed his optimism subjective. No real progress, they contended, was taking place. With her move to a regular floor, Terry's hopes were bolstered, rather than dimmed. "I know now that I've been with her thirteen or fourteen hours per day what she does do and what she doesn't do." Terry is unwavering in the belief that she is responsive, that she will eventually wake up and "walk out of here."

"She's responsive to voice. Like the other day. I'd been gone for two or three hours and hadn't said goodbye to her before I left. When I walked back in, I said hello to somebody else in the room. She was laying there, and her eyes suddenly popped open. I went over and talked to her—told her I was sorry I didn't say goodbye and said hello to her. She got a frown on her face and turned her head a little bit. She eventually warmed up and got nice with me again."

Ford says he's sure some of his assessment is still subjective. "On the other hand, it's like I told one of the clinicians the other day: if we would take their total 'objectivity' and then take what they believe is my total 'subjectivity,' somewhere in between is the answer." He says he's satisfied with "tiny little victories": the opening of an eye, the squeeze of a hand, a yawn. He's sure that each of these minute, human responses is but a prelude to 100 percent recovery. Terry's upbringing is foundation to the belief that his wife will not just survive, but prevail. As with her survival, he seems to be virtually willing her recovery. "My mother always taught me that I could do anything I wanted to do and be anything I wanted to be. She pushed that into my head for so many years while I was growing up that I've ended up believing it. Good or bad, I believe it." Coupled with this is his early religious education. By the time he was sixteen, he was a Sunday school superintendent. In Terry Ford's scheme of the world, will plus faith equals miracles.

Myer is torn between cold, clinical certainty and something deeper. He says situations like Kathy's "can be equally hard on the physicians. You get people like this who have these injuries, and you see these suffering families. In one way, you wish they didn't have to go through this any more. You know medically that she doesn't have a chance to recover. But then, you feel maybe some miracle will happen and she'll come out of this."

For most of each day, at least one family member is with Kathy. The long sessions are far from passive vigils, far removed from any death watch. They are active, interactive. In September 1985, Kathy turned thirty-six. "Delta brought in helium balloons," says Carol. We taped birthday cards all up and down an IV pole. I did that while Terry was talking to her and then I went over to her and said, 'Listen, I'm thirty-four, you're thirty-six. You're two years older than me for one month.' I harassed her about that and she made a face." Later that night, Carol walked back into the room after the party. "Her mouth was open. She would open and close it. It was almost like she was stretching. I said, 'Terry, she's going to get up in a minute!' Little signs like that mean so very much to us."

Delta has taken care of the Fords' hospital bills and incidentals. While there were still other 191 patients at Parkland, the airline maintained a command post in the basement. One by one, the patients were either discharged or died. By November, only Kathy was left. Carol says the airline provided food, a television, and companionship for the families. Marketing people and flight attendants prepared the families meals in a makeshift kitchen and tended to their every need. "They have grown close to us. They say they feel like they're our family. Even people from maintenance. It's unbelievable. They came in after working all day and stayed here until 9:30 at night."

Has the attention affected her view of Delta? Apparently. When she was scheduled to appear on a Baltimore talk show, she was initially booked on another airline. Miffed, Carol called the television station in Maryland and told them, "I want to fly Delta." "Are you *crazy*?" came the startled reply from the other end of the line. "No," said Kathy Ford's sister. "They have been wonderful to me, and I want to fly Delta. I'm very impressed with them." On her flight to Baltimore, Delta tore up her coach boarding pass and assigned her a first-class seat. During a stopover in New Orleans, several of the flight attendants gathered around her, some with tears in their eyes, and asked about Kathy. The pilot came back, offering sympathy and a cup of gumbo that he had gotten off the plane to purchase.

On the return trip to DFW, the reception was similar. "I was treated royally," she recalls. Delta found out about their special passenger on their own. She never told people whose sister she was.

Could the motivation for the special treatment be merely to keep the family from filing suit? Attorneys have suggested as much. "I don't agree," she says. "I think they're genuinely concerned." As of November 1985, the family still had not decided whether to sue. Carol says that a family she knows who did decide to file was accorded the same help as those who were still making up their minds. If there's anger on her part, it's against the legal profession, not Delta.

Not long after the crash, while there were still a number of families in the command center waiting turns to see loved ones in intensive care, an attorney walked up to Carol unannounced. "He told me who he was with and who he represented. He was asking questions of me about where I thought the largest settlements were, what courts." Was that solicitation? "He never asked for anything. He was real cool about it. He did let me know that his firm had gotten the largest settlement in a DC-10 crash. He said it was like $8 million. I was not impressed." She went to the Delta people and said, "I *do not* want to talk with him." The lawyer was asked to leave. He said he represented one of the families in the command center, and a confrontation was avoided.

A friend of Carol's told her the Saturday after the crash, "I have seen attorneys in the hallways [of Parkland]. Be very careful."

Terry's feelings about Delta are mixed. "I probably spent the first week being angry — angry at whom, I wasn't sure." When someone defended Ted Connors as not being responsible for what happened, Ford struck out: "Hey, let me tell you something. He is in ultimate command. He can tell that airport to shove it. He is in command of that heavy ship, and if he doesn't want to land it, he doesn't have to land it. He doesn't have to wait and be told what to do by some guy in the tower. When somebody defends anybody involved in this situation, I end up attacking that entity. Because they do have responsibilities. There's responsibility all over the place in this thing."

Kathy and Terry Ford were among the cream of Delta's clientele. He held one of the company's Frequent Flyer cards. Their accumulated mileage had led to free trips, hotel accommodations, and rental cars. Both belonged to the Crown Room, posh oases at the country's busier airports where business travelers could escape from long lines and crowded waiting areas. "I felt good about the way they treated you. I felt good about the airline. I really encouraged Kathy, bought her a membership in the Crown Room and all the rest of that, to fly Delta. Now I wish I hadn't encouraged her so much." As for Delta's postcrash treatment of the families, Ford feels, "They've shown a great deal of professionalism, a great deal of legitimate, sincere, empathetic concern for all the families."

In their careers, the Fords logged literally hundreds of thousands of pampered, uneventful miles, most of them on Delta. On a hot evening in August, their perspectives about air travel were forever altered. Says Terry of the circumstances that brought down 191: "Something has got to be done about this mediocrity bullshit, forgive my foul language. There's gotta be something done about it. When people's lives are jeopardized, when somebody doesn't want to be responsible — I can't handle that. Most of it is from omission, not commission. I don't think that anybody's intentionally jeopardizing safety, but the result is just the same."

Bob Sonnamaker's interest in the lady with the ring of light has, if anything, grown more intense. There's been a bonding between rescuer and patient, between EMT and family. After reading the name "Ford" in the newspaper the weekend of the crash, Sonnamaker called Parkland to find out how she was. He was told simply that she was there and still in critical condition. "I wanted to know *more*," he says, his voice rising in intensity. "I wanted to know about her burns. I wanted to know if they were able to save her foot. I wanted specifics."

As a last resort, he called the Parkland chaplain's office: "Please, give my name and phone number to a member of Kathy Ford's family. If they would like to talk to me, I would certainly like to talk to them." Within minutes, the call was returned. "I wanted the family to know that there was somebody out there who cared a lot about Kathy Ford."

As her coma persisted, Sonnamaker fell prey to depression. "I wonder, what's the use? Maybe getting to her when we did kept her from dying, but is that a blessing to the family? I don't know. A paramedic friend of mine helped me a lot by saying, 'At least you gave the family an opportunity—even if she doesn't make it—to see Kathy, hold her, and tell her they love her.'" In a barely audible voice, light years away from the boom of Big Tex, he adds, "I certainly hope she makes it."

POSTMORTEM

The identification of bodies is no mere macabre exercise. It's a legal and emotional imperative – the quicker the ID, the easier things are for the families.

The process began on the scene itself with people like paramedic Jack Ayers. After seeing that there was nothing else he could do for the living, Ayers tended to the dead.

With a small army of law officers, firemen, and other volunteers, Ayers carried out the human refuse of 191. "I don't know how many pieces of bodies that I brought out of that thing; faces, hands, feet. I remember thinking that was the first time I had ever seen a face taken off a body that was recognizable. That's the sort of stuff I haven't told anybody about. I don't say it to arouse any emotional reaction. That was how it was. That was the *way* it was."

The corporeal leavings were laid across a metal grate on the cargo ramp. Ayers was skeptical about ultimate identification: "I thought there was a significant possibility that there would be bodies that would be so finely dismembered that we would never account for them." That's the gist of what he told the Dallas County medical examiner.

For soft-spoken, professorial Dr. Charles Petty, the scene was nothing new. In fact, in contrast to some other crashes, the carnage was "comparatively" – here the word assumes the most esoteric of connotations – mild. "This is a pretty good crash to look at because the breakup of most of the bodies was not nearly as extreme as one gets with many crashes." He has room to compare. One ninety-one marked his third major aviation disaster. The highly respected past president of the American Academy of Forensic Sciences has seen it all. On a scale of one to ten, purely in terms of degree of difficulty, 191 was a "five or a six." To be sure, the ten-G impact mutilated and mangled, but it did not mince. The fire charred but did not consume.

On arriving at the east air freight area, Petty's first concern was preserving the remains. "One of the main problems was that the triage setup was established on one of the concrete ramps. They had moved those people whom they felt had some possibility of surviving onto there. Once they were found to be dead, the triage people just left them there. I think there were fifteen or so in that condition by the time I arrived. That tarmac had been heated out there over the preceding day. It had become very warm. They were cooking, they were just cooking the bodies. That was one of the reasons we wanted to get them out of there as fast as we could."

Three refrigerated trucks were summoned from nearby Grapevine to transport the dead. Bag after bag was loaded into their cold, cavernous interiors. "Live Maine Lobster," proclaimed signs on their shimmering aluminum sides. The sickly sweet smell of jet fuel and the unspeakable contents of the plane mingled with the acrid smell of smoke as stone-faced volunteers gently loaded the trucks. All the while, helicopters circled, their sunguns flooding the killing field in a ghastly flat white light. It was like a scene from an improbably horrible science fiction movie.

As the trucks were unloaded at the Department of Forensic Sciences behind Parkland, the painful, painstaking process of identification began. Some fifty physicians, dentists, and assistants gathered at the large, antiseptic-looking building. Later, Delta personnel and an eight-member FBI disaster team joined in. They formed the nucleus of a round-the-clock task force charged with bringing surety to those who still lived with—in some cases clung to—uncertainty. With official identification of the dead, denial—one of the classic stages of grief—could itself die.

Although identification was often arrived at after tortuous forensic examination and comparison, with one category of victim it began more simply. "We were lucky," says Petty, "in that most of our bodies—I won't say they were intact—but the majority of them could at least be recognized as people, not just pieces of people. Now, some were badly beaten up, of course. But many of them could be recognized. What you do is start taking those people and see what there is that you could possibly identify by simply looking at the individual."

58 Immediately, the victim was examined for clothing type, jewelry, surgical scars, and amputations. "In some instances, we were quite lucky. The man would have in his coat or pants pocket a billfold that had his driver's license and maybe several photographs of him which you could look at and say, 'Gee, this really must be the person we're talking about.' Now, that's not really positive identification, but it's enough to get the body out of the normal channel of processing into the [category of] 'We think we know who this guy is.'" Petty says that two teenagers were identified simply by names sewn into the waistbands of their underpants. "I assume they were on their way to camp."

Sometimes appearances deceive. A wallet that was culled from the scene clearly belonged to a body. The question was, which one? Visual references to photos in the billfold convinced forensics officials that they had a match. "He was almost a deadringer," remembers Petty. "When you look at his photograph and you look at the body, you think, 'This is one and the same.' It turned out not to be. So you really can't go on this. You have to go on more positive identification."

With 191, there was a second category of victim that defied even preliminary visual ID. "Their clothing's pretty well torn off and there doesn't seem to be any jewelry," says Petty. "You can't really look at them and tell who they are. You have to go into a secondary form of identification." That means dental records and fingerprints. And delays.

One ninety-one crashed late Friday afternoon. For more than sixty hours, the bureaucracies—private and governmental—that store the structure of our smiles and sworls of our fingertips were closed. California, the home of a number of passengers, presented a particular problem. When a California resident gets a driver's license, a thumb is printed. Petty wanted access to the records. "They were shut down and weren't about to open up," he remembers. The weekend's work, although not wasted, was hobbled. It wasn't until noon Monday that the medical examiner's office could tell California officials what prints to look for. "Then, you've got the delay in going into the files and finding them. You're not looking for electronic files, now. You're looking for *paper* files." Still, Petty says officials were cooperative.

Even in instances where strong preliminary identification had been made, something more positive was needed. For those whose dental records couldn't be located or who had no fingerprints on file, a bit of detective work was called for. In one case, Petty says, "We had fingers that we could print, but no fingerprints to compare with. We were able to develop a print on a prescription form." The form was in the luggage of the person whom pathologists presumed that person to be. It matched.

In an earlier crash Petty worked on while he was in Maryland, forensics experts obtained the same kind of match by going to a victim's home and taking a print off a cold cream jar. In the wake of disaster, people's personal habits—how they brush their teeth, even how often they dust the furniture—can sometimes haunt foren- **59** sic specialists. So immaculately clean was one victim's home that Florida police had to go over the place for five hours before finding her prints. "This is the sort of thing you have to do," insists Petty. "You can't do a thing, however, if you have a body and haven't any idea who it is." This is why he says that pathologists working on the 191 crash were "lucky." In most instances, they had a place to start, be it a wallet, a ring, or, as a final resort, a passenger list.

Still, lists often lie. An airplane is more than a means of conveyance; it can be an escape machine. To program for the latter, you have merely to feed the airline inaccurate information. "As far as we know," says Petty, "there was no substitution of one person for another on the plane – a man traveling with his girlfriend under his wife's name or something like that."

The only passengers not listed by name on 191 were innocents, young children. They clustered right around two years of age. "The airline lets you fly a child for free up till two, and they'll kind of warp that a bit. People will say the kid's two when he's actually three." The upshot was that there were three victims not registered on the list.

Remarkably, the passenger manifest of Delta 191 was virtually devoid of intrigue, mistake, or misnomer. Petty says that last-minute substitutions on commercial airliners occur all the time. He was once one himself: "When I was in Louisiana, another man was due to go to a meeting when his child came down with meningitis. He called and said, 'Look, I've got the tickets. I can't go. Do you want to?' I said, 'Yeah, I'd love to.' He said, 'If you can get out here before we leave for the hospital, you can have the tickets. That left me about two hours to get on the plane. There were no changes of name. I went under 'Dr. Davis.' "

"The other substitution I've seen at airports – I do a fair amount of traveling – on a couple of occasions I've seen a cabin crewmember, a flight attendant, say 'Oh my God! I'm glad you could get here.' The other woman runs into the cabin just before they close the door and they change spots, for whatever the reason. Perfectly legitimate. An unscheduled change. I've seen that go on a couple or three times."

This is one of the reasons why Petty was especially anxious to identify the flight attendants as quickly as possible. "These people all looked about the same. They're chosen for their height and so forth. Anthropometrically, they have to meet certain standards." In the case of 191, all the attendants were women. "Sex, size, and uniform – all the same," says Petty. "They're uniform all the way down. It's kind of an interesting phenomenon."

The last two bodies positively identified were flight attendants. "We had a terrible time figuring them out," says the medical examiner. "They [Delta] do not fingerprint their flight crews. I think it was an executive vice-president of Delta who said they stopped doing that because there were objections on the part of the people who were to be fingerprinted, stating that it was an invasion of their privacy." Petty considers the policy "a mistake. In the Air Force, you have fingerprints on file. Footprints too, because they learned by sad experience that Air Force pilots frequently wear fairly heavy shoes and that the feet tend to stay intact where the hands don't in crashes."

For the families, the wait for positive ID was excruciating. By 8:30 a.m. Sunday, August 4, 49 of the 133 initial fatalities had been identified and 40 families notified.

Petty says the process was speeded up by a computer manned by airline personnel. An electronic network established by Delta's insurance carrier eventually linked officials in thirteen states and Australia with Delta representatives in the conference room of the Forensic Sciences building. Slowly at first, then in a rush, the etchings of earthly existence came in: X-rays, dental charts, fingerprints. There were photographs, too, of pretty young women in summer white dresses and fathers in the prime of their lives. They were compared with what lay below, in the cool tiled confines of the basement.

When a cousin of mine died in the crash of a Braniff Electra in 1959, a friend of the family's traveled to a place called Buffalo, Texas, to identify the remains. The visage that lay draped on a hardwood floor in the high school gym seared the friend, shaking him as nothing had before, not even hellish remembrances of trench combat in World War I. With 191, officials say—to their knowledge—no relatives physically viewed the bodies. A medical examiner's staffer says, "We try to do that by answering their questions as fully as possible, so they won't feel a need to go beyond that discussion."

On Thursday, August 8, some five and a half days postmortem, the last of the victims were identified. Eighty-eight primary IDs had been made by comparing dental records. In 94 instances, dentition also served as positive confirmation. Fingerprints accounted for 77 primary IDs, 45 total; physical descriptions for 22 primary, 87 total; and X-rays for 3 primary, 3 total. Ultimately, 130 bodies were identified by the Dallas County medical examiner's office. They were subject to 229 examinations. Two crash victims were identified by the Tarrant County (Fort Worth) medical examiner. The 133rd initial victim—the driver of the Toyota on Texas 114—was identified early on.

For Petty and staff, the task exacted a physical and emotional price. "You learn to handle it the best you can," says the scholarly ME. "I spent some time yesterday here with the wife of one of the people killed. I was pretty emotionally involved by the time she left. I was, in a sense, sharing her grief with her. But that's part of the game. That's what any physician does. Some of our people had a little bit of a problem, but I don't think it was major."

The medical examiner's job was over. By now, the physical product of August 2 lay in the hands of others.

"**W**e're not demanding anything. We just want our share." The speaker is a mortician. The subject is bodies.

Accusations of racism, favoritism, and body hustling flashed across the screen August 5, as some twenty angry Dallas funeral home owners confronted David Clayton, president of the Texas Funeral Directors Association. Acting on a phone tip from the owner of a minority funeral home, a Channel 8 camera crew was on hand at the Dallas County medical examiner's office as Clayton defended his decision to allow only seven area funeral homes to handle the earthly remnants of the victims of 191. The list included one of Clayton's own properties, as well as six other funeral homes scattered around Dallas County.

"It's a shame that now, with a hundred and thirty bodies, we have to sit down here and have a discussion of what we're going to do," said a surprised and somewhat angry Clayton. "There's no way to invite everyone into the process."

The Texas Funeral Directors Association was involved in the crash from the very beginning. In June its Disaster Committee had held a seminar at DFW. The idea was to plan for the unthinkable, to draw up a worst-case scenario for the coordination of airport personnel, the Department of Public Safety, the medical examiner's office, and morticians. Michael Goggans was chairman of that committee. He never dreamed he would be putting into action in August what he had sketched out in June. The plan worked well and quickly. Even as rescuers searched the wreckage for the living, funeral home workers sifted it for the dead.

"We had crews out there in shifts," remembers Goggans. "We would take crash bags and tag the bodies as a white male, black female, whatever." This was intended to make initial processing at the morgue easier.

Singly and in pairs, the innocuous-looking refrigerated trucks arrived at the medical examiner's office. Don McElroy, owner of Dallas Mortician's Service, was at the ME's office that Friday evening for another reason. He had to pick up the body

63

of a woman killed in a traffic accident. McElroy's firm isn't a funeral home. He doesn't deal with the public. At the request of a funeral home, Dallas Mortician's will pick up, embalm, transport, and ship a body from Dallas to the receiving funeral home, be it out of town or out of state. Shortly after dark, as McElroy pulled up to the entrance of the medical examiner's office, two of the seafood trucks had just backed up to the loading dock.

"I immediately saw what was going on. You could smell the jet fuel, the burned odors. . . . I've been around this business all my life. I was in the army mortuary service." McElroy knew he was witnessing the aftermath of some major disaster.

He walked around to the back door. Several morgue attendants and clerks stood mute, peering into the back door of one of the death trucks. They seemed stunned, horrified by the sheer volume of the carnage.

The bodies were in black disaster pouches, each lying on a backboard. They had been put in two deep. During the trip from the airport, some of the bags had torn.

McElroy assessed the situation, then climbed into the charnel chamber. "What are you going to do?" asked the horrified bystanders. Responded McElroy, "You've got to get them out, don't you?"

Inside, it was cold and dark. McElroy, dressed in the uniformly somber suit of his chosen profession, leaned over and went to work. "I just got up in the back of the truck. One of the truck drivers was helping me. We were actually having to stand on body bags so that we could start to get these bodies out." There were no lights in the truck, but those from the cameras of the media helped a little.

McElroy and the driver began handing bodies to the morgue attendants and clerks. A deputy sheriff arrived and joined in. As more hands arrived on the scene, a grim human conveyor belt developed. All twenty-five or thirty of the black pouches were unloaded from the first truck.

With the arrival of subsequent deliveries, more volunteers appeared. The owners and several employees of a small funeral home came over to see if they could help. McElroy contacted his staff, and soon there were "about eight or ten of us unloading the bodies."

64

"We had bodies all over the morgue. We worked another two or three hours unloading all those bodies. We unloaded three trucks, probably seventy-five, eighty, ninety bodies we unloaded." McElroy and his team worked into the wee hours of the morning.

Dr. Petty and his staff immediately began the process of identification. By 4 a.m., eighteen to twenty victims had been matched with a name. The bags to which names had been afixed were stored in a special forty-foot trailer in the parking lot. It too was refrigerated. There simply wasn't room in the morgue anymore. By now there were half a dozen workers left, some paid, some volunteer. McElroy made sure that the identified remains were placed in the truck side by side, to make things less confusing for the funeral homes.

Exhaustion began to take its toll. Word came in that there was another forty-foot trailer waiting on the tarmac at DFW. It was due to arrive shortly. An impromptu meeting of staff and volunteers decided it would have to wait.

McElroy collected the remains of his traffic accident victim and went back to the office to begin embalming the body. By 7:30 a.m. it was ready for shipment home. He cleaned up, took a shower, and fell asleep. Thirty minutes later, the phone rang. It was an out-of-state funeral home, asking if he would handle the body of one of the crash victims. Don McElroy's professional involvement with 191 had begun.

While McElroy was unloading bodies, David Clayton was at a banquet in Austin, honoring a past president of the Texas Funeral Directors Association. His first word of the crash came in a phone call from his wife. Clayton had confidence in Disaster Committee chairman Goggans's ability to handle the situation. He stayed in Austin, updating members of the association on the crash. Clayton returned to Dallas at midday, Saturday, August 3.

He found the Disaster Plan in place and functioning smoothly. Goggans had been notified, had gone immediately to DFW and taken charge of removing, bagging, and transporting the former passengers of 191 to the morgue.

Clayton met with Goggans and asked him what should be done next. Goggans told him that Delta had contacted a man named Samuel Douglass in California. Douglass too is a funeral director, owner and manager of several California facilities. He is considered an expert on air disasters, having been involved with thirteen of them over the past decade and a half. Douglass was due in that evening. Goggans had already arranged a nine o'clock meeting at the medical examiner's office.

While waiting for Douglass to arrive, Clayton and Goggans attended to details: lining up more disaster pouches, contacting casket manufacturers to arrange for the large volume of "merchandise" mandated by the contents of those pouches.

At that initial meeting, Douglass outlined Delta's criteria. Topping the list was visible respect. He wanted all remains to be picked up and delivered, one at a time, in hearses. Funeral directors handling the victims should be prepared to pick up the remains at the medical examiner's office, treat them, casket them, and deliver them to DFW for the flight back home.

Past experience indicated that identification could drag on and on. "I came prepared to stay six weeks," Douglass told Clayton. "I have no way of knowing how long it will take to identify all the remains, clinically treat them, and return them to a receiving funeral home."

Because of all that was involved, said Douglass, "You need to choose firms that have a large enough staff that can support us over an indefinite period of time

65

and still carry on their day-to-day routine in their normal trade territory." He also wanted to make sure that those chosen to do the job had the equipment to do it right.

In his mind, Clayton began to tick off the names of firms with enough space, hearses, and staff to handle the load. He already had a pretty good idea, but he told Douglass, "Let me meet with them, and I will confirm a list to you by 10:30 or 11:00 in the morning." Douglass agreed.

On Sunday evening, Clayton began calling funeral directors, inviting them to gather at Anderson-Clayton Brothers in Mesquite. His list included representatives of Laurel Land, Restland, and Singing Hills (all owned by the same company), Cedar Crest Funeral Home, Lamar & Smith, and Weiland Funeral Directors. All agreed.

The meeting of five people representing eight firms was "probably the shortest I've ever been in in my life." Clayton outlined the situation, explained Douglass's criteria, and told those assembled that he had volunteered their services (there was a $10,000 budget for the TFDA Disaster Committee to cover such eventualities). Still, he said that Douglass, on behalf of Delta and the insurance carrier, had insisted on setting a fee. "It was set by Delta and was not arbitrated in any way. It was accepted, and not even discussed. For most of the firms," says Clayton, "it was probably less than they normally charge." Everybody was willing to help, saying they would wait until the medical examiner started releasing bodies. Meanwhile, they would get ready.

As Clayton returned to the ME's office, his list of recommended firms in hand, McElroy's solitary work continued. He was well into processing his third crash victim and had already arranged shipment of the body back to Los Angeles Sunday evening. Looking down at the papers on his desk, he was struck by the irony of it all. The container and its contents would be loaded aboard an L1011 TriStar, Delta Airlines Flight 191 to Los Angeles.

McElroy was following up on a fourth call from an out-of-state funeral home when he ran into a brick wall. He called the ME's office to leave the name of the victim and request that he be notified as soon as positive ID was made. His contact, a longtime acquaintance, told him about the list. It was official, and McElroy wasn't on it.

McElroy was confused. What list? David Clayton's list, came the reply: no authorization, no body.

McElroy asked for the names of the approved firms and got them. He knew that Clayton was president of the Texas Funeral Directors Association, but he did not see how that gave him the authority to decide unilaterally who would and would not deal with the human remains of 191.

Irritated, McElroy wanted to talk to Mike Goggans. Perhaps he could tell him what was going on. Goggans confirmed that, yes, there was a list, and no, Dallas Mortician's Service wasn't on it. McElroy's firm didn't meet the criteria, one of which was the possession of a Cadillac funeral coach.

A police officer stands near the burning debris of Delta 191. (*Dallas Morning News,* Ed Sackett)

Artist's depiction of the plane's descent and crash. (Chris Butler, *Dallas Times Herald*)

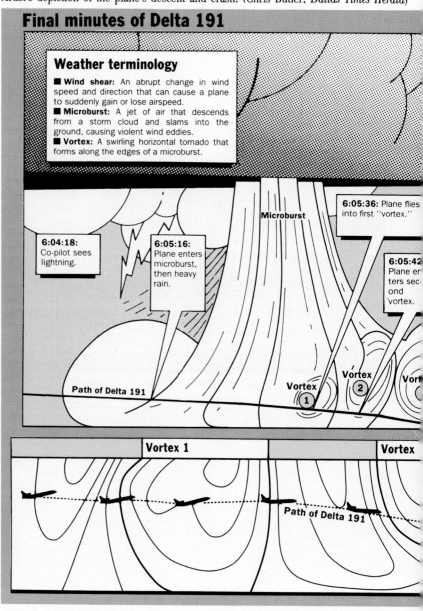

Final minutes of Delta 191

Weather terminology

■ **Wind shear:** An abrupt change in wind speed and direction that can cause a plane to suddenly gain or lose airspeed.
■ **Microburst:** A jet of air that descends from a storm cloud and slams into the ground, causing violent wind eddies.
■ **Vortex:** A swirling horizontal tornado that forms along the edges of a microburst.

Microburst

6:05:36: Plane flies into first "vortex."

6:04:18: Co-pilot sees lightning.

6:05:16: Plane enters microburst, then heavy rain.

6:05:42 Plane enters second vortex.

Path of Delta 191

Vortex 1

Vortex 2

Vort

Vortex 1

Vortex

Path of Delta 191

These diagrams depict the storm encountered by Delta Flight 191 as it approached Dallas Fort-Worth International Airport about 6 p.m. Aug. 2. The storm contained a "microburst," or thick column of turbulent air extending down from a thundercloud. Curling around the column were a cluster of "vortex" spheres that contained violent, swirling downdrafts, updrafts and cross-currents. As shown in the diagram, the Delta L-1011 crew, after first seeing lightning, flew through the shaft of the microburst and then through three vortexes before touching down in a field a mile short of the runway.

The diagrams and flight path were plotted by T. Theodore Fujita, a professor of meteorology at the University of Chicago with the assistance of Delta Air Lines. His analysis, issued recently in a report titled "DFW Microburst," are based on radar and satellite data, ground-based measurements and computer analyses of the plane's digital flight data recorder.

ane enters third

6:06:01: Collision with water tanks.

Impact

■ **6:04:18:** Co-pilot Rudy Price, eying clouds, says, "Lightning coming out of that one." Airspeed 150 knots.

■ **6:05:03:** Plane hit by headwinds.

■ **6:05:16:** Plane enters microburst.

■ **6:05:19:** Heavy rain begins falling. Capt. Edward Connors tells Price, "Watch your speed." Airspeed increases to 173 knots. Altitude 700 feet.

■ **6:05:21:** Connors: "You're gonna lose it all of a sudden." Plane hit by tailwind. Airspeed drops to 159 knots.

■ **6:05:25:** Connors: "Push it up, way up." Airspeed is 140 knots.

■ **6:05:27:** Connors: "Way up." Airspeed is 135 knots.

■ **6:05:28:** Connors: "Way up." Airspeed still dropping.

■ **6:05:29:** Flight engineer Nick Nassick: "Way up." Airspeed 129 knots.

■ **6:05:30:** Connors: "That's it." Airspeed increases to 133 knots as plane begins recovering.

■ **6:05:35:** Airspeed rises to 139 knots, a safe speed for that stage of landing approach.

■ **6:05:36:** Plane enters a powerful "vortex," a tornado-like cell of swirling air, and is hit by a strong updraft and lateral gust. The plane rolls from side to side, then is hit by a strong tailwind. Connors: "Hang on to the s.o.b." Airspeed drops to 120 knots, and co-pilot applies full power. Plane is at 500 feet.

■ **6:05:40:** Strong downdraft hits plane. Plane starts to drop below glide slope and nose, which had been tilted up at 15 degree angle, starts to drop.

■ **6:05:42:** Plane enters second, less powerful vortex. It continues to descend and nose is pointing down at a 8½-degree angle.

■ **6:05:44:** Ground proximity warning sounds: "Whoop, whoop, pull up."

■ **6:05:45:** Connors issues order: "TOGA" (take off, go around). Plane now at 250 feet.

■ **6:05:47:** Unknown voice: "Push it way up." Pilot gets plane's nose pointed up slightly.

■ **6:05:48:** Plane penetrates third vortex and is hit by a strong tailwind.

■ **6:05:50:** Plane leaves vortex, with nose slightly downturned.

■ **6:05:52:** Plane touches down in field 6,300 feet north of Runway 17-Left.

■ **6:05:55:** Unidentified voice: "Oh (expletive deleted)," as plane bounces, hits car on Highway 114 and shears off five utility poles.

■ **6:06:01:** Plane slams into airport water tower.

Vortex 3

A priest administers the last rites to crash victims. (Jim Gallagher, *United Press International*)

Emergency medical personnel and police at the crash site, where bodies are lined up near the plane wreckage. (*Dallas Morning News*, Jim Burton)

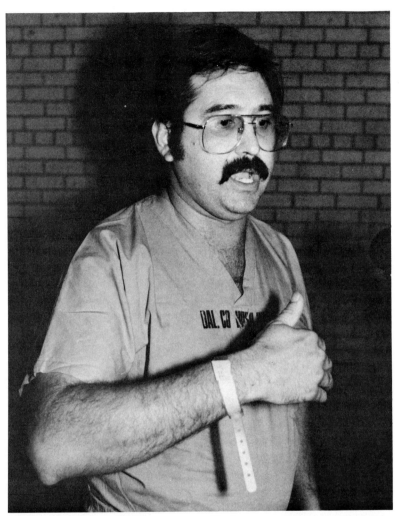

Johnny Meier, a Delta 191 passenger, outside the emergency room of Parkland Memorial Hospital in Dallas. Meier was returning to his home in Temple, Texas, following a business trip to Florida. He led rescue efforts of surviving fellow passengers and managed to carry half a dozen crash victims to waiting ambulances. (*Houston Chronicle*, Larry Reese)

Captain Edward M. "Ted" Connors, Delta 191's senior officer. (Courtesy of Delta Air Lines)

Rudolph P. "Rudy" Price, Copilot. (Courtesy of Delta Air Lines)

Nick N. Nassick, Flight Engineer. (Courtesy of Delta Air Lines)

Leora, Annie, and Dana White at home.
(Jerome Chandler)

Ron White. White had just been
promoted to buyer for a major Dal-
las/Fort Worth nursery chain when he
left on his first business trip. (Courtesy
of Leora White)

The Kaiser family. Robert, Karen, Kandace, and Kathryn, September, 1984.
(Courtesy of Karen Kaiser Clark)

Kathy Ford and other sales representatives for Reynolds and Reynolds are honored at a "300 Club" meeting at Sandpiper Bay, Florida, 1981. She was the first sales rep to be admitted to this elite group of sales achievers after only six months on the job. (Courtesy of Reynolds and Reynolds, Grand Prairie, Texas)

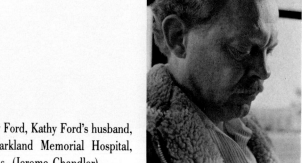

Terry Ford, Kathy Ford's husband, at Parkland Memorial Hospital, Dallas. (Jerome Chandler)

Dr. Dan Meyer, Kathy Ford's physician at the time of her initial admission to Parkland. (Jerome Chandler)

Bob Sonnamaker, at home. Sonnamaker was driving a friend to DFW airport when Delta 191 went down. Trained as an Emergency Medical Technician, Sonnamaker made his way to the crash scene and began searching for survivors. He was the first to discover Kathy Ford. (Jerome Chandler)

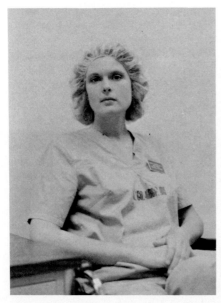

Pam Walter, Head Nurse at Parkland's Burn Unit. (Jerome Chandler)

Dr. Charles Petty, Dallas County Medical Examiner, at his office. (Jerome Chandler)

A crash victim arrives at Parkland by helicopter. (*Dallas Morning News*, Bill Roth)

A microburst embedded in the rain shaft from a thunderstorm near Stapleton International Airport in Denver, Colorado, July 6, 1984. (National Center for Atmospheric Research)

AIRBORNE WIND SHEAR WARNING SYSTEM. Safe Flight Instrument Corporation's computer, with synthesized voice alert, warns the pilot of the presence of hazardous, low altitude wind shear, or microburst, before aircraft performance loss becomes critical. The system is operative on both takeoff and landing approach. (Courtesy of Safe Flight Instrument Corporation)

Gene Skipworth, air traffic controller who cleared Delta 191 to land, at National Transportation Safety Board hearing. (Jerome Chandler)

Rufus Lewis, pilot of the Learjet immediately preceding Delta 191 on runway 17L, at National Transportation Safety Board hearing. (Jerome Chandler)

Burnelli Lifting Body Design

Artist's conception of proposed Burnelli "lifting body" jet airliner. (Courtesy of The Burnelli Company, Inc.)

Fuselage
Structural Weight

15%

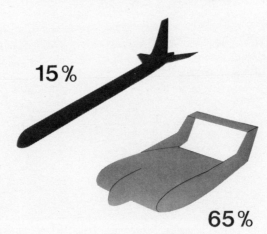

65%

This view of a proposed Burnelli airliner highlights the "box body" strength of the craft as compared to that of conventional airliners. (Courtesy of The Burnelli Company, Inc.)

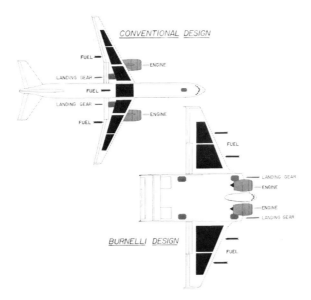

An overhead view of a Burnelli as compared with one of a conventional jet transport. Note the outboard placement of fuel tanks, away from the passenger compartments. (Courtesy of The Burnelli Company, Inc.)

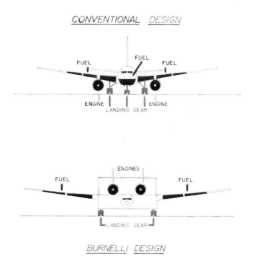

Head-on view of a Burnelli "lifting body" airliner. Note that compared to a conventional jet airliner, the Burnelli fuselage itself contributes to lift; hence the name, "lifting body." (Courtesy of The Burnelli Company, Inc.)

The remains, it was explained, had to be casketed. Since McElroy didn't deal with the public, he usually didn't use caskets, preferring instead to use containers specially designed for shipping. He left casket selection to families and receiving funeral homes. The policy was reflected in his fee, which was significantly less than it would have been with casket included. Further, McElroy was given precise specifications for the caskets that would be used: 20-gauge monoseal and manufactured by a specific company. Two colors would be used: blue for women, bronze for men. Finally, as a matter of decorum, Delta required that each of the caskets be delivered to DFW individually, in hearses, for shipment home. It may have been a mass tragedy, but the response would be as personal as possible.

Dallas morticians handling the bodies were also expected to provide the receiving funeral home with all necessary paperwork and arrange for shipment via Delta. Billing would be through Anderson-Clayton Funeral Home. A delay of sixty to ninety days was expected before payment. The fee had already been set by Delta and accepted by those on the list.

McElroy didn't see how anyone could provide all that and still make a profit at the fee set. Aside from that, he felt that it had become a matter of principle. Don McElroy, independent Dallas businessman for more than a decade, felt that he was a victim of discrimination, shut out by members of his own fraternity. The big boys had taken over the game, preventing other players from even entering the ballpark.

McElroy phoned several other small independent homes and services. None had been invited. Each felt as McElroy did: they should have been included, or at the very least, consulted. Some were members of the TFDA, but many belonged to the Independent Funeral Directors Association of Texas, a smaller group whose membership is mostly black. To Don McElroy's way of thinking, not only was the little guy getting a raw deal, but so were minority firms. He got on the phone to set a meeting with Clayton.

At the medical examiner's office, identification was moving faster than anyone had dared hope. Legally, some necessary paperwork had to be issued from the jurisdiction in which the crash occured. To streamline this process and speed the remains back to the families, Clayton proposed that a sort of branch office be established at the medical examiner's. The presiding judge concurred. Certified copies of death certificates (when available), burial transit permits, and other incidentals could be taken care of in consolidated fashion. Delta personnel would aid in the identification process and the shipping of remains via a computer link. Instead of running all over the county, morticians could take care of business in a single stop. Clayton was on his way to pick up the clerk who would run the field office when McElroy called. Clayton explained what he was trying to do and said he would meet with McElroy and the others in about an hour.

When Clayton and the clerk arrived at the ME's, McElroy and his group were already there. So was Channel 8, a fact that Clayton did not like at all. Negative publicity was the last thing he wanted, and public disagreement among funeral directors was bound to result in negative publicity. Long years of dealing with people under stress had taught Clayton the truth in the cliche, "It's not so much what you say, but how you say it." There was no way either group could come out of this thing looking good.

Clayton took his time getting the court clerk settled in her new office space, hoping that McElroy and the others would think things over and cool down by the time he reappeared. They all represented local firms. Clayton knew everybody there. Surely, he felt, once things were explained to them, they would have better sense than to create a scene in front of the camera.

When David Clayton emerged from settling the clerk, he entered an emotionally charged atmosphere. Don McElroy was mad, demanding to know by whose authority Clayton had dreamed up the rotation list. Murmurs of angry assent rose from the morticians. More than anything, Clayton wanted a chance to have his say away from the invasive camera. He spoke to the people from Channel 8. They were polite and cooperative, agreeing to let Clayton speak to the group in private and return only if invited.

After the television crew backed off, Clayton explained that he had more or less just assumed the authority to deal with the Delta representative. After all, Douglass was an expert in these matters, had been contacted by Delta, and had followed his standard procedure by contacting the representative of a large funeral director's association near the site of the crash. The TFDA was large, he was its president, and the Disaster Committee was in place and functioning. Time and the feelings of the families were the major considerations. There had not been time to contact every funeral home in the city to see if they could meet the criteria outlined by Douglass. As for McElroy and the other mortuary services, they couldn't be included on the list because they are legally constrained from dealing directly with the public. Further, explained Clayton, any firm specifically requested by a receiving funeral home would be contacted and treated with the same respect and courtesy as those on the rotation list. "We've got folks standing in line at bloodbanks, we've got physicians at Parkland—they're having to send them home because they're in each other's way there are so many. *Please* don't embarrass yourselves or our profession by creating a controversy now," Clayton implored.

Verbal oil didn't smooth troubled waters. The media was invited to return. Several of the angrier comments were repeated for the benefit of the churning minicam.

"We use Delta airlines," said the owner of a small, black funeral home.

"There were black passengers aboard that airline, and I think it's only fair that if we patronize them, they should patronize the black community. I feel that he is discriminating against my firm and all of the other firms in the city of Dallas that want to be on this rotation list."

Stung, Clayton responded, "I'm sure that our judgment can be questioned by anybody. But the basic decision that was made was based on trying to help the families that are in Florida and California, and heaven knows where, to get their loved ones back to them as quickly as possible."

One of the unmollified morticians countered, "I feel the reason I wasn't contacted is because of greed. Flat greed. I've been in this business for a few years, and I've learned that the funeral directors—funeral homes are probably one of the most greediest [sic] professions there is." More accusations of greed and racism flew, but over all the commercial cacophony was the voice of Don McElroy, demanding to know, "Are you denying us the opportunity to be on this rotation list?"

Clayton's control snapped. He was tired and frustrated. He had the unmistakable feeling that the situation was getting out of hand. He turned to McElroy, who was speaking loudly about legality and fairness. "I understand you shipped a body illegally, with a Dallas permit rather than one from Irving," said Clayton deliberately. When the story was edited for presentation, McElroy's counter to the charge was covered by the narration of the reporter. McElroy denies shipping the body illegally. He says he received a proper burial transit permit from the Dallas Bureau of Vital Statistics, adding that at the time he shipped the victim home, the medical examiner's office wasn't yet set up to issue the permits. In any event, no charges have been filed against McElroy.

Channel 8's report was picked up nationally. Viewers of the evening news were treated to the spectacle of a group of angry undertakers fighting for the human leavings of Flight 191. "The gist of it was that funeral directors were arguing over the bodies," says Clayton ruefully. "Mr. Douglass and I held a press conference on Friday afternoon after the last remains were identified. All of the networks were there, several radio stations, print media. It got ten seconds on Channel 8's five o'clock news. The networks didn't pick up anything."

At the conference, Samuel Douglass commended the medical examiner's office and the TFDA for "the most efficient disaster operation" he had ever seen. "During the twelve to fifteen years that I have worked with disasters such as this, I have never seen one handled as efficiently as the one here in Dallas." Douglass said it usually takes up to three weeks to identify and ship the bodies in the wake of a major air crash. With 191, almost everything was taken care of within a week.

A check of the WFAA news script of August 9 shows that the press conference received considerably more air time than Clayton remembers: one minute and thirty-five seconds, to be precise. Clayton's explanation of the circumstances surrounding the controversy were clearly presented, as was Delta's praise of the cooperation between the medical examiner's office and the funeral homes.

While David Clayton is miffed that the speed and efficiency of his operation were not widely disseminated to an incredulous public, Don McElroy feels that—at least where he's concerned—word of a different kind spread like wildfire. "My business has drastically dropped since this," he says, hands folded and head bent. "I normally run about ninety calls a month. Last month [August 1985] I only did about forty-five. I don't deal with the public. I deal strictly with funeral directors. They pass the word around. I feel that word is already being passed around: don't use Don McElroy."

Clayton denies any knowledge of a deliberate blackball attempt. Both men have received calls and correspondence from across the country. "I have answered every one of those letters," says Clayton. "Without exception, when I gave them all the facts, all the details, they've said to me, 'Had we known the facts, we wouldn't have written.' "

McElroy feels that he has suffered unjustly, in part because he sees himself as an entrepreneurial David to an institutional Goliath. But there is more to it than that, says the silver-haired man with the proper wire-rimmed spectacles. "People don't want to think about death. They think, when something like this happens, 'These guys are out there jumping on the situation to get all these bodies and make all of this money.' That's not true. But the public thinks it is, because this is a closed industry. Funeral directors and their associations have kept this [industry] closed from the general public. They don't want the general public to know what they do."

Clayton and McElroy both proudly display letters from Delta, thanking them for their help in the wake of one of the most efficiently handled disasters in history. Each mortician feels that his efforts were misunderstood, unappreciated by the other. Clayton is planning to attend every regional association meeting of his organization in the state of Texas, to tell them "what really happened."

McElroy says simply: "It takes a unique type of individual to do this for a living."

Within hours after it went down, 191 was well on its way to becoming a cottage industry. Media, morticians, and lawyers: each jockeyed for the emotional, earthly, and legal leavings of August 2.

Of these, perhaps the most lasting images are of the attorneys. In the days following the crash, families of victims were contacted unbidden, a three-column ad was run in a Dallas newspaper (on the same page as crash stories) noting specialities in air crash and wrongful death cases, attorneys paced the halls of Parkland, and the son of the "king of torts" checked into the Hilton Inn. Overnight, DFW became a hot market for the handful of lawyers across the nation who specialize in litigating aviation accidents. Depending on your perspective, they are either avenging angels or avaricious adventurers.

Hal Monk personifies the old-time Texas lawyer: salty, quick, sagacious. In the course of his fifty-three years, he has worked as a crew member on the world's largest bomber, a newspaper reporter, an insurance investigator, a bureaucrat, and executive assistant attorney general for the state of Texas. Along the way, he managed to pick up a private pilot's license and 2,000 flying hours. He does not fit the buttoned-down, BMW mold of yuppie advocate.

The morning after the crash, as Monk recalls it, the phone rang in his suburban Fort Worth office. It was Melvin Belli, the larger-than-life San Francisco trial attorney. Monk had worked with the controversial barrister before. Belli said his answering service had received a message from a man whose family was on 191. Belli was supposed to return the call to the Hilton Inn after 9:45 but wasn't sure whether the person meant Dallas or San Francisco time. "If he wants to talk to us," Belli asked Monk, "would you be in a position to go out and see him?" Monk said yes. Belli said he would check back later, after he talked with the man. Shortly before noon, the phone rang again. Belli "was livid," says Monk. "He said, 'I started to try to call the man at 9:45 our time and the operator [at the Hilton] wouldn't put the call through. I kept trying.

Now, the hotel operator has finally admitted to me that the reason she wouldn't put the call through to that room was that she has instructions from Delta that they are not to put through any calls to these families from any lawyers. They're screening my calls! [Hilton denies this.] Will you get out there and see what the hell is going on?' "

The hotel was fifteen minutes away. "I'll go out there and either talk to your client [actually a *prospective* client at this point] or get thrown in jail trying," responded Monk. He wrote down the man's room number, got in his car, and headed east toward the hotel. When he arrived, "I didn't go through the switchboard, the desk, or anything else. I went right to the room." The person had left just before Monk arrived. He talked to some other family members who had gathered in the room and told them that Belli had been trying to get through. One of the family, says Monk, replied that they were talking on the phone to Belli at that very moment. Satisfied that he had done his job, Monk left.

Saturday evening, Monk checked with Belli again. "He was not in a very good mood," remembers Monk, "not in a good mood at all." It seems that the family had actually been talking with his office, not with Belli himself. Lawyer and potential client hadn't made contact. Belli was irritable. He would dispatch his son Caesar and associate Richard Brown to Dallas to "talk to those people [the family that had called] and see if they want to hire us." The younger Belli and Brown would arrive at DFW Sunday. Could Monk meet them at the airport and make hotel arrangements? From past experience in working with the Bellis, Monk says he remembered that they preferred Hiltons. Anyway, the address would be convenient.

Monk says that after Caesar and Brown arrived, they contacted the man who had called. "Just wanted to let you know we're here," they said. "Call us when you're ready to talk about it." No push, insists Monk. No hustle.

That's not the way Dallas saw it. A bit of background: In 1964, in a Dallas courtroom, Melvin Belli defended one Jack Ruby for the murder of Lee Harvey Oswald. Although Ruby's conviction was ultimately overturned, San Francisco sophisticate Belli lost the trial itself. He was beaten by the then– and now–district attorney of Dallas County, earthy, cigar-chomping Henry Wade. Before returning home in defeat, Belli waxed bellicose, leveling a scathing indictment against the city and what he called "Dallas justice." Now, twenty-one years later, his son was back, a visible player in the most emotionally wrenching event to hit the city since the Kennedy assassination.

The comings and goings of the Bellis have been the stuff of headlines for years. Perhaps the most famous recent excursion was to Bhopal, India, in 1984 in the wake of the toxic chemical disaster that claimed thousands. "They accused me of 'chasing ambulances' in Bhopal," retorted the "king of torts" after his widely criticized journey. "I don't have to chase ambulances. The clients come to me." And so it was, according to Monk, at DFW.

72

Soon after the story that Caesar was in town hit the local media, Monk says the phone started to ring. Most of the calls were from the Hilton. "People who couldn't get any specific answers [from Delta] started calling the Belli suite. They'd want to talk. I'd certainly be less than honest with you if I didn't say that all of us there had some hope that if the people were impressed that we helped them, we knew what we were doing, we were competent in the area, they might want to hire us." Ultimately, more than half a dozen did.

Texas Governor Mark White, from August 3 a visible figure in postcrash news, told reporters that the Texas State Bar should prosecute attorneys who engaged in solicitation of cases involving the crash. The state's seldom-used barratry law says: "A person commits an offense if he solicits employment for himself or another to prosecute or defend a suit or to collect a claim (or) procures another to solicit for him employment to prosecute or defend a suit or collect a claim."

Monk flatly denies that the Belli group solicited clients. "As to the question of knocking on doors in hotels, if this had been a truckload of migrant farm workers that had been injured, maybe knocking on doors might have got some business. But people on airplanes are basically not stupid, and I can't think of anything that would piss people off any more than for a lawyer to have initiated contact in a hotel out there. I mean, aside from the impropriety and grossness of it, I just can't see that he [Belli] would have benefited. In some instances, we told them on what basis we represented people in this situation. We didn't ask anybody to sign a contract. We did *show* people what our contracts consisted of." And the fee? "I remember one case that did talk to us brought up pretty seriously about our fee. Our response was, if we wind up with several of these cases, it will be 20 percent [of the recovery]. Otherwise, it will be 25 percent. I frankly think that in one of these mass disaster cases anything over one-third [contingency fee] is unconscionable."

It takes money, lots of money, to litigate a major air crash effectively. Belli's firm, as with many others when there's a major disaster, often joins in a consortium of general and aviation attorneys. Expenses are shared, and so are fees. Going it alone, the family lawyer can quickly find himself faced with staggering outlays and for-midable opponents—such as United States Aviation Underwriters (which manages United States Aircraft Insurance Group).

73

United States Aviation Underwriters, Delta's insurer, is one of the foremost underwriters of commercial aviation liability insurance in the United States. It is also perhaps the most controversial. Within twenty-four hours after 191 went down, Monk says that the company's senior vice-president and director of claims, Robert L. Alpert, was on the scene "giving Delta instructions about what to do." Some of those instruc-tions, Monk contends, were designed to effect "claimant control" of survivors and fam-ilies of victims. He concedes that while Delta's assignment of representatives to each family was motivated largely by compassion, there was more to it than that. He said that representatives were told, in effect, " 'Find out everything you can [about your charges].' USAIG started building their dossier on each prospective claimant, I'll say by Monday morning after the crash on Friday." Was this part of an intelligence operation by the insurer? "Precisely," says Monk. "In a lawsuit, information is power."

Robert Alpert says that insurers traditionally arrive on the scene immediately in the wake of a crash, primarily to offer assistance in expediting body identification. "We did not give Delta any 'instructions,' as the term appears to be used here, with respect to what to do with the individual relatives." Alpert says that the Delta representatives were there solely to give aid and comfort to bereaved families. As for the compilation of dossiers on potential claimants, Alpert says, "We do gather information on the people from the day the accident happened." He bridles at the notion of the process as an "intelligence" operation.

In a letter dated August 27, USAIG told at least one of the victim's families, "You may be entitled to a substantial sum of money under the law of the jurisdiction which will ultimately be applicable in this case. We are writing you to obtain certain information which will assist us in evaluating the loss you have sustained. It would be extremely helpful to us, and we believe beneficial to you, for you to provide us with the requested information. It is our intention to see that you receive fair and prompt compensation for the loss." The letter goes on to request things such as the annual salary of the victim, his or her general health, relationships, and the employment status of next of kin. In addition, it says, "You may wish to consult your *family* attorney or business advisor for guidance or assistance in this matter" (author's emphasis).

Monk and others believe that the reference to the "family attorney" is no mere folksy touch. Major plaintiffs' attorneys say that USAIG *wants* local, general-practice attorneys to negotiate settlements. In referring to a case being handled by his consortium, Monk says, "USAIG will pay a million dollars on that case pretty early on. They'll do it. On the other hand, if Hal Monk—lawyer in the cubbyhole suburb of Bedford, without any connection with any of the name lawyers—were to go it alone, there's no way I could get 'em up over—they'd dig their heels in about $600,000 and probably wouldn't pay a dime more till we got to the courthouse steps."

San Francisco's Gerald Sterns is one of the country's eminent aviation attorneys. Among the cases he has litigated are the jumbo-jet collision at Tenerife, the PSA midair collision at San Diego, and the infamous Turkish DC-10 crash outside Paris. Sterns argues that families are especially vulnerable immediately after a crash. "The big risk in this is that the victim, who is really not in a position to deal intelligently with insurance companies or with Delta Airlines or Bob Alpert or any of those people, is likewise in no position to deal intelligently with what lawyer they're going to select."

Sterns, like Monk, feels that the family lawyer who did a superb job of drawing up your will is simply outclassed when it comes to tilting against people like USAIG. "Here's a guy that's got a license to practice law. Legally – unlike the medical field where you're not supposed to do brain surgery until you've practiced it – legally, the day after this kid gets his ticket, he's a fully licensed lawyer. He can appear in any court in the state and he can try a major airplane case. There's nothing to prevent him from doing that."

Sterns argues for specialty certification within individual states, something akin to board certification to practice a specific type of medicine. He doubts that it will ever happen. When multimillion-dollar pies drop out of the sky, everybody wants a piece.

Despite the reference to "family attorneys" in their letter following the crash of Flight 191, USAIG has adopted a more subtle approach to families than it did after notable crashes. A case in point is the crash of Pan Am Flight 759 in Kenner, Louisiana. An isolated microburst was also the killer of 759. This time, it struck on takeoff. One hundred fifty-three people died when the fully loaded 727 slammed into a quiet residential neighborhood near New Orleans's Moisant International Airport. In a letter dated July 14, 1982, USAIG wrote to families of victims on the ground. It said, in part:

"It is also our hope that you ultimately retain as much of the compensation as is properly due you without unnecessary diversion of large amounts of legal expenses. You may find yourself under pressure to sign a contingent fee retainer with an attorney whereby his fee is a percentage of the final award. The rationale for such a percentage fee is that the lawyer risks getting no fee if there is no recovery. There is no such contingency in this case. *There is nothing to be gained by a precipitous lawsuit*" (author's emphasis).

The letter, signed by Alpert, angered some plaintiffs' attorneys. Mutual wariness between insurer and a number of aviation tort lawyers continues to this day.

Following 191, some plaintiffs' attorneys believe that USAIG has increased the amount of its initial settlement offers as compared with past crashes. Hal Monk says the insurers "have somewhat come into the twentieth century." On the high end, the family of one $60,000-per-year breadwinner who left a wife and two children was reportedly offered $1.5 million. On the other end of the scale, the family of a victim with two nondependent children was offered only $150,000. While the size of the proposed settlements for 191 is higher than in past crashes, Monk adds, "The best offers I have heard about would be acceptable only if the plaintiff is in very strained economic circumstances."

Alpert counters this way: "The trend – if there is any trend – is that our offers, since the early 1970s, have been *exceptionally* consistent with the jury verdicts that are being returned in the cases in which we make offers."

75

FIRE & RAIN

After the 1977 collision between two 747s at Tenerife, USAIG was responsible for more than 360 of the 644 claims that resulted from aviation's worst-ever disaster. Alpert says that of the more than 360 claims, only 9 went to trial on the issue of damages. He says of those 9, "In every single one of those cases, our offers were proven to be consistent with jury verdicts. In each one of those cases that was tried, the victims—the passengers on the airplane—got less money by going to court, hiring a lawyer, and waiting two years [for trial]."

Alpert believes that the acid test for recovery is straightforward: "What was offered by U.S. Aviation. The date it was offered. What was [eventually] obtained and *how much*—this is the most important question—how much did the *client* get of all that was recovered? There's a very big fallacy in our legal system: if you wait three, four, five, *six* years, the jury verdict will almost always be greater than the original offer." The USAIG executive says that contingency fees charged by attorneys and lost interest —interest that could have been accruing, had the insurer's initial offer been accepted —significantly dilute the ultimate return to claimants who choose to go to court.

Insurance companies would seem to be understandably interested in limiting settlements. Through the first three quarters of 1985, statistics from Lloyds of London indicate that aviation insurance companies expected to pay out some $830 million worldwide in liability and aircraft hull damage claims. This compares with about $300 million for all of 1984. As a result of the mid-decade carnage, the International Air Transport Association estimates that insurance premiums for the aviation industry could rise 40 percent. There is talk of developing airline-owned insurance carriers to deal with the escalating costs.

Gerald Sterns says the actual figures paid out by aviation insurers in individual cases are closely held secrets. "The insurers are not anxious to publicize that information." The best he can offer is an estimate based on comparing notes with other aviation attorneys. "In rough figures, the last number that seems to be agreed upon is that the average settlement number on a domestic crash is probably in the range of $350,000 per seat." The figure covers a myriad of different situations. The common thread that runs through them all is the loss sustained by the survivors, economic and otherwise.

Says Sterns, "You have two fellows sitting side by side on the aircraft of identical age and earning capacity. They could be working for the same company. One leaves a wife and five children. One is a bachelor whose parents are dead. In the five-children case, you'll probably have a million-dollar loss. In the other, you have zero because there is no dependent heir to claim the loss. You average those two together, and you have $500,000. Average amount paid out and top dollar are two different things."

The top dollar has been rising in recent years. The crash of another Flight 191, an American DC-10 in Chicago, resulted in a string of seven-figure death verdicts rendered by juries. The plane was full of businessmen. That, and inflationary times, sparked the quantum departure from past air crash settlements. Gerald Sterns: "Say you've got a fellow in his late thirties or early forties making $30,000 per year. He's got a wife and two or three kids. That's a pretty typical profile. Say he's thirty-five. He's got thirty years of working expectancy. Assuming inflationary and merit increases in his pay are offset by discounting to present value based upon the investment rate, then you have a $900,000 economic loss. If the plaintiff's lawyer is able to convince the jury that inflation is going up faster than the investment rate, then it could be a million, million-two, million-three." In the profession, these are called "work-life expectancy" calculations. "*Then* you've got the loss of the family relationship, which is certainly worth something. Arguably, you're looking at a million and a half dollars' worth of damage."

Assessing "noneconomic loss" is the most emotionally volatile element of the macabre equation. In effect, the jury fixes a dollar value to the destruction of the family unit. Sterns offers a hypothetical example based on the shootdown of Korean Airlines Flight 007. Based on "work-life expectancy" calculations, a forty-year-old businessman earning $50,000 per year and leaving a wife and three children could reasonably expect his case – were he around to see the proceedings – to bring his family $1.25 million, less legal fees.

Suppose that sitting next to the man is a young woman, single and supporting only herself. She's a world-beater. "The sun rises and sets on her as far as her parents are concerned," says Sterns. "She's a kind and loving daughter. She's a microbiologist and she's going to do wonderful things. She's going to find the cure for AIDS. But she's not supporting anybody."

Because the craft was shot down on the high seas, Sterns believes that Maritime Law will probably apply. That means families would be entitled only to provable economic loss. In a lawsuit, the family of the businessman would receive $1.25 million, while the bereaved parents would get nothing.

Were the law of other jurisdictions applied, California for example, the result could be decidedly different. The woman would be subject to that state's law concerning loss to society, which allows juries to place a value on intangibles. If there is a way people can monetarily measure the essential worth of another human being, this is it.

"The jury instructions still say it's the loss to the survivors," says Sterns. "But you and I know better. This does give the jury a chance to praise the human being as to what kind of person they were. I remember a case that came out of the Grand Canyon crash years ago [a 1956 midair collision in which 128 people died]. The lawyers are still talking about that one. Some guy, it turned out, had three wives. No one could tell for sure who was his real wife. His life was pretty muddled." Sterns says that the jury liked neither the dead man nor his wives. The verdict was for three dollars—one dollar per "spouse." He contrasts the finding with a recent one in New York where the family of a young scientist who died on American Flight 191 [the DC-10 crash in Chicago] was awarded some $7 million. The havoc wreaked upon his family and his worth to society transcended the cold mechanics of "economic loss."

Major air crash case litigations are broken down into two phases: liability and damages. Proving the former can be—although it certainly isn't always—the "easy" part. Recovering the latter can prove to be a legal labyrinth. Sterns says liability in passenger air-carrier crash cases is "really a slam dunk. Somebody's screwed up."

It becomes a "slam dunk" only after considerable pushing and shoving under the backboard, however. Typically, defendants make concerted efforts at shifting the blame—the airline to the FAA, the manufacturer to the airline, and so forth. When the plaintiffs have done enough work to make further protestations by the defendants futile, the resolution of fault becomes a straightforward matter. Indeed, it is often admitted by the defendants before trial. Sterns believes that one of the main advantages in employing a competent, experienced plantiff's attorney is that he can "bring that case to bear much more quickly. We know exactly what we're doing. We know exactly whose button to push and how to get Delta and the United States (of America) on line in a hurry to start paying those claims. Otherwise, they'll screw around forever, particularly the United States government. There's no end to the bullshit they can pull." Still, the issue of liability is ultimately resolved in most cases. "Then the question becomes, how much do they have to pay? At this point, you're dealing with multimillion-dollar decisions, i.e., whose law is controlling."

Following the crash of 191, many of the lawsuits were filed in Florida, California, and Texas. A breakdown of residency for the deceased passengers shows why: sixty-eight lived in southern Florida, twenty-one in southern California, six in the San Francisco area, three in Atlanta, four in North Texas, four in other parts of Texas, five in Utah, two in Colorado, seven in other states, and one in Australia. Separate trials in each jurisdiction would prove costly and impractical. By late November, thirty-seven lawsuits had been filed in eleven different courts with twenty-five different law firms. It was up to the federal Judicial Panel on Multi-District Litigation to make jurisdictional sense of the legal matrix. The nine-member panel met in Portland, Oregon, to decide where the cases should be consolidated. It chose the court of United States District Judge David O. Belew, Jr., of Fort Worth. "Centralization . . . in the Northern District of Texas will best serve the convenience of parties and witnesses and promote the just and efficient conduct of this litigation," the panel's order read.

The choice of Belew, who had recently undergone surgery for cancer of the colon, came as a surprise to some attorneys, Hal Monk among them. Still, Monk says, "of all the judges in the Northern District of Texas, I think he probably would be my first or second choice." Belew was appointed to the federal bench in 1979 by President Carter.

The Northern District of Texas will determine who was at fault in the crash of 191. But consolidation in a particular state for purposes of determining liability doesn't automatically mean that that state's law will apply when it comes to the awarding of damages.

Judges can look at a number of different factors in deciding whose statutes control: the domicile of the decedent, which jurisdiction has the greatest interest in the case, and which jurisdiction has the most significant contacts with the case. When the significant-contact theory is followed, the options become mind-boggling. A large percentage of the passengers on 191 came from Florida; many were on their way home to California; the L1011 was manufactured in California; Delta is based in Georgia; the accident happened in Texas; the FAA and National Weather Service are based in the District of Columbia.

It is in the damages phase, in the pretrial trenches, that plaintiffs' and defendants' attorneys do the fiercest battle. "The bucks that are at stake are just phenomenal," says Sterns. "With a big planeload of people, if a defense operation can convince a judge to apply the law of state X as opposed to state Y, it can literally save tens of millions of dollars."

In the case of the Turkish DC-10 near Paris, an improperly designed rear cargo door blew out of the craft, causing the floor to collapse. The control systems to the elevators were severed, and the ship dove to its death. Three hundred forty-six people died. They came from thirty-four foreign countries and seventeen states. Federal Judge Pierson Hall of the Central District of California heard the landmark case. In determining whose law should control for damages, Hall rejected the domicile theory. He said that it would be unfair and unreasonable to ask the jury to sift through the statutes of fifty-one jurisdictions, that the domicile of the victims was strictly providential, that the plane was built in California, and therefore California's wrongful-death statute should hold sway.

The ruling "probably cost Lloyds of London [the lead insurer] $100 **79** million," says Sterns. Although Hall's decision to apply the law of the defendant's home state is considered by many aviation attorneys to be the leading opinion on the subject of controlling law, in subsequent crashes its application has been less than universal.

While the passenger manifest of American 191 at O'Hare was made up largely of businessmen – breadwinners – the composition of Delta 191 was more demographically varied. A number of retired people, some families, and a smattering of children made the flight representative of society as a whole. Many of these "noneconomic" victims were from Florida and Texas, two states with among the most liberal personal injury laws in the nation. Both jurisdictions permit substantial federal-income-tax-free recoveries for the emotional loss sustained when a child or elderly parent dies.

On the face of it, either the law of Texas or that of Florida would seem equally advantageous to claimant families. But statutes don't tell the whole story. Juries usually determine the dollar amount of recovery, and juries can be quirky. Hal Monk says, "In terms of the elements of damages that you can recover for, Texas is one of the best jurisdictions. On the other hand, our juries tend to squeeze a nickel till the buffalo shits in the Indian's face."

Subsequent to August 2, Delta Airlines was hit by a number of lawsuits. In turn, Delta filed a third-party complaint against the United States of America. Specifically, the carrier alleged that the crash was "proximately caused by the negligence of one or more air traffic control personnel employed by, and acting within the course and scope of their employment with, the FAA." Delta wants the federal government to bear part of the financial burden of any recoveries. In response, the FAA denied any wrongdoing.

When is the government legally at fault? With one notable exception, the "sovereign" (i.e., the federal government) is immune from suits. That exception is the Federal Tort Claims Act. Passed in 1946, the act permits the United States to be held liable to the extent that a private person would be held liable under the law where the act or omission occurred. There is no one standard of liability for the government. There are fifty, one for each state. On the face of it, the federal government would seem as vulnerable as anybody else. "That's the large print," smiles Gerald Sterns. "As they say in this business, 'The large print giveth, the fine print taketh away.' "

Governmental authority is exercised in essentially two ways: through discretionary actions and through ministerial actions. Says Sterns, "Anytime a government official is exercising his discretion—rightly or wrongly—the government is immune. That's called 'discretionary immunity,' and the FAA raises it in every single case." The courts have fairly well defined the line between the two as far as air traffic control is concerned. If a controller tells a blip on a radar scope to turn right instead of left and a crash ensues, he negligently exercised a ministerial function and can be sued. "But," cautions Sterns, "if the FAA decides not to install Doppler Radar—even though they have it in the state of the art and have been screwing around for ten years—that's discretionary." In other words, the FAA can choose to install equipment or impose a rule—at its discretion. Once the choice is made, the equipment has to be employed properly and the rule followed; a discretionary decision becomes a ministerial mandate.

The upshot for the flying public is that if you are going to get at the FAA, it has to be via an individual negligently exercising a delegated ministerial function. An individual cannot sue the government for a series of administrative decisions – no matter how callous – leading to the failure to deploy life-saving equipment or promulgate rules designed to promote safety.

A recent Supreme Court ruling has narrowed the government's window of vulnerability even further. On July 11, 1973, a Varig Airlines Boeing 707 bound from Rio de Janeiro to Paris crash-landed at Orly Airport. One hundred twenty-four of the 135 people on board died from asphyxiation or the effects of the toxic gasses emitted from the burning interior. The in-flight fire originated in a lavatory waste bin. A federal regulation in effect at the time the 707 was certificated by the then-CAA (now FAA) mandated that waste receptacles be made of fire-resistant materials and that they incorporate covers for containing possible fires. In a suit brought under the Federal Tort Claims Act, Varig charged that the CAA had negligently certificated an airplane that did not meet its own regulations. The theory was that the CAA may not have had to make a rule, but once it did, it had the responsibility to make sure it was followed – straightforward logic with which the Ninth Circuit Court of Appeals agreed in finding for Varig and against the government. According to the Supreme Court, "The Court of Appeals viewed the inspection of aircraft for air safety regulations as a function not entailing the sort of policymaking discretion contemplated by the discretionary function exemption."

The reason the 707's waste bins got by was that the CAA inspected the craft via a "spot check" method; not every item on every plane was scrutinized. When the Supreme Court heard the case, it agreed with the government's contention that it was protected by discretionary immunity. Varig lost, and so did the flying public. The Court's rationale for the ruling was that Varig's contention that the CAA/FAA was negligent in failing to inspect the bins "necessarily challenges two aspects of the certification procedure: the FAA's decision to implement the 'spot check' system of compliance review, and the application of that 'spot check' system to the particular aircraft. . . . In our view, both components of respondent's claim are barred by the discretionary function of the Act."

81

The High Court went on to say that "in administering the 'spot check' program, these FAA engineers and inspectors *necessarily took certain calculated risks* for the purpose of advancement of a governmental purpose and pursuant to the specific grant of authority in the regulations and operating manuals" (author's emphasis).

To cap the controversial decision, Chief Justice Warren Burger wrote, "The FAA has a statutory duty to *promote* safety in air transportation, not insure it."

The Supreme Court of the United States has not yet blessed air traffic control with a bureaucratic blanket of discretionary invulnerability. Still, Sterns and others are worried about what they perceive as a trend in High Court decisions, worried that further emasculation of the Federal Tort Claims Act could prove to be one of the bloodiest, yet least obvious, blows to aviation safety yet.

COCOON

In the days immediately following the crash, something unplanned and unprecedented happened. In the guise of an airport hotel, an intimate community was spawned – a place where people could cry, care, comfort, and be consoled.

From the outside, there was nothing unique about the setting; it was just another upscale business habitat whose normal population craved little more than a night's respite from the commercial wars, a decent dinner, and a wakeup call in plenty of time to catch the next flight out. The staff of the DFW Hilton had always been adept at catering to those kinds of needs. In the week that followed the crash of Flight 191, they would learn to provide for other things.

Delta picked the Hilton to house the handful of ambulatory survivors and the families of those who had died. Some 150 of the 400 rooms were blocked off, including the entire eighth floor. Within a week, the hotel had become a haven, a hideaway where it was acceptable to be a child again. A cocoon.

Bob Hicks is a forty-year-old professor at Dallas Theological Seminary. The Methodist minister and father of three is the type of guy who immediately puts strangers at ease. During his seven years in Hawaii, his pastoral work had concentrated on marriage and family. He is a Christian for whom compassion counts more than creed.

A chaplain in the Air National Guard, Hicks rose early on Saturday, August 3. When he arrived for weekend duty at the Dallas Naval Air Station, his commanding officer assigned him to the Hilton. Another officer in Hicks's unit, a Delta employee, had been busy for the past several hours setting up a command post at the hotel that would take care of an influx of bereaved and disbelieving families. Delta was paying for the entire thing: airfare, lodging, food, and sundries. But it immediately became clear that more was needed than simply sequestering people while they steeled themselves for the officially pronounced fates of their mothers, fathers, sons, and daughters.

FIRE & RAIN

When Hicks walked into Delta's temporary offices on the third floor, he was given the job of organizing a massive ministerial effort. "I grabbed the nearest Red Cross worker," Hicks remembers, "and said, 'We're going to need priests, rabbis, and any other ministers you can get out here.'" The initial job was the toughest: accompanying Delta representatives as they delivered death notices. "They were asked to do an impossible job with no training, no knowledge of trauma, no background. Many of them just flat didn't believe they could do it."

Most families who checked into the Hilton that Saturday were suspended somewhere between hope and disbelief. Even though the list of survivors had already been released, they had "the hope that *their* loved one was still wandering around someplace dazed, at the hospital, in the emergency room." Most wanted to go immediately to Parkland, even the crash site, in the prayer that some bureaucratic sin of omission had left the most important name of all off the list of living. Denial, the first classic stage of grief, ruled the day. Before final acceptance of what had happened, there would be anger, depression, and even bargaining with the Almighty. But first, there was the prevading sense that this just could not be.

"A tragedy like this quickly brings to the surface everything that is going on in our lives," says Hicks. "The greater the relationship, obviously the greater the grief." And vice versa. "There were some people celebrating in their rooms at the expense of Delta and having a wonderful time, saying 'Well, I may as well take care of the funeral arrangements and drink the free booze.'" Most relationships were built of stronger stuff—enduring, solid, and shattered by a shear of wind.

As Saturday became Sunday, families found their own private spaces, huddling together in the lobby, at a corner table of the Wickerbasket restaurant, or simply staring vacantly at the blue flicker of a television set. Grief was a personal thing, precious and solitary. Another manifestation of the beast, anger, began to assert itself. Nurtured by self-imposed isolation, it sullenly stalked the corridors looking for victims.

Sunday night, the ministerial team arranged for an interdenominational service in a hotel conference area. Eighty people showed up, carefully distanced little knots of people spread throughout the room.

84

A rabbi gave an Old Testament reading, Hicks one from the New. A priest led the liturgy. "We asked a couple of the families if they would offer prayers, read scripture, be involved in the service. Several of them broke down. But it was great, because it said to everyone else: 'It's okay. We all feel the same way.' Some even prayed out their anger toward God." When the service broke up, the hallway filled as stranger embraced stranger and in doing so absorbed one another's losses. For the first time, these once-removed victims of 191 acknowledged the sorrow around them. "Our prayer and goal for that evening was a corporate sharing of grief." And so it was.

Karen Kaiser Clark recounts the atmosphere that pervaded the place during the ensuing week: "What we did was to get up and wander in the lobby waiting for word. We'd watch and visit with other survivors." Tears and touching, tenderness and total vulnerability were all totally acceptable. "My husband tells of a man walking in the lobby and all of a sudden his shoulders started to tremble as if he were crying." Lou Clark went up to the other man and hugged him. For five minutes, two grown men stood in the middle of a busy hotel, weeping as they embraced. Finally, the man said, "I'm okay now. I just needed someone to hold." Neither traded names.

The Book of Romans says, "Weep with those who weep." In the wake of 191, Bob Hicks tested the limits of Paul's injunction. In his dealings with families, Hicks tried to get people to talk about those who had died. One way was to ask for pictures, snapshots of life sandwiched between credit cards and driver's licenses. Hicks remembers one man in particular. Both his wife and his child were on the plane. He proffered the picture of his wife sadly. But when he pulled out that of his youngster, "It all came out. We just cried. I was crying." Growing up in Kansas, Hicks lived by the conventional wisdom that as a man he had to be immune, strong with those who wept. Mass tragedy vanquished the residue of his earlier conditioning. "You just find yourself weeping. Therapeutically, it's the best thing you can do."

Some people embrace the counselor while shunning the cleric. In negotiating the emotional mine field of the Hilton, Hicks understood this. "We don't have to play a spiritual game here," he told people. "It's okay to grieve. It's okay to be angry. Later, let's get together and talk about the role of faith and your religion in this whole process. But now is really not the time."

When it came, prayer was often in the form of the question, Why? Why does one person walk away from carnage without a scratch while it takes medical examiners the better part of a week to even identify the person who was sitting across the aisle? Why? "I don't have the answer for that," sighs Hicks. "I wish I did. It's at points like that I would say, 'Would you care to pray, or would you mind if I prayed?' In my prayer, I would say 'Lord, we don't know why; and we're angry we don't know why.' "

As the week wore on, "we had a couple of families realizing that perhaps their loved ones might not be identifiable. The remains were so—gold and silver had melted out of the teeth. The teeth were gone and all the fingerprints were burned." One such family, still in the throes of denial, asked to be taken to the killing field so that they would be assured of a memorial service. "That's one good thing funerals do, give that sense of finality that the person is dead," says Hicks. It releases the "pause" button and enables people to get about the business of living.

When the little group pulled up to the scene in a Delta van, the media had already gotten the word. The visual impact would be extraordinary. Minicams came to life as photographers adjusted their unblinking boxes for white balance. Hicks says that, among others, NBC was there. "We had to tell them that this was very private.

85

This was family." They wanted to know what family. "We wouldn't tell them."

Hicks, a Red Cross worker, and a Delta representative pulled back from the picture. The family walked through the blackened entrails of the L10, occasionally pausing to kick a piece of wreckage or stare to the north. Finally, the Delta employee gently pointed out the section of the great craft where the person had been sitting. Someone asked, "Why don't we do it here?" Forming a circle, they gathered hands. As they committed a soul to the Almighty, a plane on final approach to runway 17L flung the light of the summer sun back to the heavens from which it came.

There were other families for whom a trip to the killing field was essential. Dallas psychiatrist Dr. James Black told the *Psychiatric News*, "We walked to the site of the crash. We could still smell the fuel, see the water tanks the plane hit before it came to a standstill. Intelligence has nothing to do with mourning and talking about it in a doctor's office is sometimes just not good enough."

Before the pilgrimage to the scene, Black had asked Delta for something else: an L1011. "They didn't ask me a question in the world. They just pulled one up to the terminal."

The destination of this particular flight wasn't to be found on any timetable. The idea was to transport the family from confusion to comprehension. They were having trouble dealing with death. "The only visible mark the relative had from the crash," said Black "was a scar on his face. That was all. The family couldn't understand why he had died when all they could see was a scar. So I took the family on the plane and had them sit in row 28, where their relative sat. I explained to them that no one who had sat up to fifteen rows behind this area had survived." Sitting in the seats, looking out the windows, feeling the fixtures, they finally understood.

Black, a private practitioner who teaches at the University of Texas Health Science Center, learned Saturday morning that "Delta was understaffed and getting into trouble at the Hilton." Accompanied by a medical resident, he hurried to DFW. During the next few days, hotel became hospital as Black and ten other psychiatrists "made the rounds." He termed the Hilton "a fascinating psychiatric setting." Delta picked a place that was at once isolated and intimate. It was removed from the bustle of Dallas and out of sight of the charred tombstone-like tail of the TriStar. At the same time, it was convenient to DFW.

The families who wandered into the lobby in tow of their Delta representatives were, said Black, "in a regressed state, and it was easy to exercise parental control." They were suggestive to direction, something that in another setting might have seemed patronizing. Some wanted to identify remains, even though there was precious little recognizable. A gentle "no, that's not a good idea" helped.

What could have been "an aggressive, angry situation" became something very different, believes Black. The Hilton became an island in the storm. Families didn't have to venture into an unknown city to identify or claim bodies. They didn't have to go to Parkland, where "a variety of different kinds of losses would be experienced." Instead, these other victims of 191 could – in a very real way – go home again. "Families found togetherness," said Black, "recalling their lives as children with a mother and father when all their material and now emotional-religious needs were met. This environment resembled a loving, protective, early developmental phase in people's lives," a cocoon.

On occasion, the world managed to penetrate. "One morning, when we couldn't find my mother," remembers Karen Kaiser Clark, "I read the paper. The coroner responded to an inquiry as to what the people [crash victims] looked like. He said they looked like 'charred little rag dolls.' At that point, I closed the paper and cried. I couldn't read any more, *because that was my mother.*"

The Tuesday morning after the crash Karen lay in bed, wrapped in a cocoon of her own: "My husband was still sleeping. I thought to myself, 'If I wrap the covers tight enough, maybe I'll be safe.' " It was then she knew she was in trouble. Against the most primal pull, she forced herself to get up and shower. Needle-like spray scoured away the suffocating warmth of semisleep. "I went straight down to the counseling center. I walked in and asked if I could use the phone, because it was still hard for me to say, 'I can't cope anymore.' " She dialed a friend. The answering service clicked on the line, cold, impersonal, and far away. Kathryn Kaiser's eldest broke down. "A psychiatrist came in and asked if I would like to talk. I said, 'I need to very much.' " For two and a half hours, there were tears and the exorcising of fears.

Black believes what happened that week may herald "a new era in psychiatry. It could even be helpful in setting up programs for large firms to deal with trauma, for example, a mine cave-in. Industrial accidents are going to continue, and psychiatrists are well attuned to dealing with them."

James Black's work, provided to those at the Hilton free of charge, isn't over. What happened there may have lessened somewhat the postcrash problems of survivor's guilt, flashbacks, and nightmares, but they can still recur.

Chaplain Bob Hicks worries about those things, too. "From my experiences as a pastor, there's immediate comfort and support for the first couple of weeks after everyone gets back home from the tragedy and the funeral. But after about a month, everybody gets back to work and a normal routine." That's the toughest time, between one month and six months after the loss. "The support is no longer there," says Hicks. "Then you really are alone. Totally alone."

Six weeks after the crash, Hicks sent out a pamphlet on grief to those he met at the Hilton. He has also made personal follow-ups. One ninety-one is still very much with him in a way that nothing else probably ever will be. "I've had to deal with grief and dying and cancer and those kinds of things before. What I've learned from this is that mass trauma is totally different from individual trauma." In the past, Hicks could go to the hospital, deal with death, even weep with patient and family. But then he could go home, turn on the television, have dinner, and work on the following Sunday's sermon. The ability to compartmentalize is central to making a go of the helping professions: police, fire fighters, doctors, and clergy. "But this was different," says Hicks softly. "I couldn't go home. I couldn't teach. When I tried, the people, the faces, the imagery were still there. You can't walk away from it."

On the Monday following the crash, after a short sleep and before returning to the hotel, Hicks drove to the seminary's East Dallas campus. His eight o'clock class was a straightforward affair, a subject he could teach almost from memory. As he sat down and opened the notes, nothing happened. He just stared at them, incomprehensible hieroglyphs. Closing his eyes for a moment, he looked up and said, "Look, I don't know what's wrong with me. I just don't think I can get through this today." A long pause: "Most of you don't know where I've been this weekend. Let me tell you." As he began to speak of the unspeakable, he broke.

Bob Hicks's own grieving had begun.

A DEATH IN THE FAMILY

For many of the 37,000 employees of Delta, grief was personal, not merely corporate. The airline had quietly boasted one of the best safety records in the industry. It had been twelve years since a company craft had gone down—on July 31, 1973, when a DC-9 on a fog-shrouded approach to Boston's Logan International Airport had crashed into a seawall. Eighty-nine people died. Prior to that, Delta had gone twenty years without a passenger fatality. In 1953, one of its DC-3s crashed in East Texas, killing sixteen.

In 1985 Delta's ad campaign reflected both its record and its innate conservatism. While other airlines chased each others' tails in the postderegulation dogfight for customers, alternately touting lower fares, more legroom, and free trips, the Atlanta-based carrier's message was simple: "Delta Gets You There." The four-word slogan spoke volumes, not just about frequency of scheduling and available destinations but, more subtly, about trust: ride with us and you'll get where you're going. Safely.

For many domestic airlines, real cost-cutting was a crash-course phenomenon, one born of unbridled competition from new entrant carriers like People Express, Air Florida, and others. Delta and another major domestic carrier, Minneapolis-based Northwest Orient, had always been frugal. At Delta, paper clips are recycled, company memos are written on the backs of used envelopes, and a special committee meets regularly to approve any departmental expenditure over $350. "We're not a budget operation," says Jim Ewing, the airline's director of national media relations. "The money doesn't go out without approval." The pinch-penny policy doesn't apply to flight operations (maintenance). That department gets what it needs, when it wants it —no questions asked. One longtime FAA official in the southern region says, "Delta has the highest maintenance standards in the industry, bar none."

The company's ledger books and stock prices reflect its conservative approach. Exactly one week before 191 went down, word came from Delta's board-

89

room that all previous records for both operating and net income had been broken. Net income for fiscal year 1985 was $259.4 million, up 48 percent from the previous fiscal year. Operating income was $366 million, a 73 percent gain over 1984's figures. The debt-to-equity ratio, a key yardstick of airline health, was an enviable 29 percent debt to 71 percent equity.

A number of factors contributed to the record: good economic health for the country as a whole; increased traffic; new markets such as Paris, Frankfurt, and Honolulu; and lower fuel costs. All these helped. But what underpinned the numbers, Delta claims, was its people.

Virtually everybody except flight crews starts out on the bottom rung at Delta. Before you become a marketing representative, you work behind the counter. Before you dispatch airplanes, you load bags. Hiring is a selective thing; company people recommend people they know for employment. Critics call it "inbreeding." Competence alone won't land you a job. Nor will membership in a union. Only two unions have managed to gain a foothold in the world's fourth-largest airline: the Air Line Pilots Association and the Professional Airlines Flight Control Association. Labor problems, which almost brought Eastern and Pan Am to their knees, historically haven't existed at Delta. Some competitors privately claim that the "family" spirit that supposedly permeates the airline is Pollyanna pap. Others charge that Delta is paternalistic. "I think there's no question," smiles the angular, crew-cut Ewing. "We're paternalistic as hell! We're just as paternalistic as can be, from start to finish."

Freedom from union work rules, Delta officials maintain, boosts productivity. Territoriality and the rigidity that goes with it is minimal. Once, a delayed clean-up crew threatened to delay a flight from La Guardia to Atlanta. The L1011 was a mess. Old newspapers, dirty headrests, and full ashtrays abounded. Passengers impatiently waited to board, most of them businesspeople with appointments to keep. The senior flight attendant walked out the jetway, looked around the lounge, and spotted two senior company officials. She grabbed them and put them to work. They doffed their coats, rolled up their sleeves, and grabbed a couple of portable vacuum cleaners. The plane left on time. One of the passengers was an industrial psychologist. "I'm not believing what I'm seeing," he said. "Didn't you guys just get on the airplane and clean it up?" "Sure did," said one of the execs. "There's nothing we won't do to get these planes out on time."

The airline business is a cyclic thing, its peaks and valleys made more pronounced by the uncertainties of deregulation. Historically, when business is bad, people get laid off—furloughed, in airline parlance. The experience often leaves a bitter taste in the mouths of pilots. I remember vividly the reaction of a member of my family when he was furloughed by a major West Coast carrier. Before finally being recalled, he puddle-jumped from an obscure commuter airline to crop-dusting to aircraft sales – hardly terra firma upon which to build a family. The experience left him cynical. The residue for his company was a skeptical work force. Furloughing has only happened once at Delta, when twenty-six pilots were laid off for six weeks. In recent years, when business was bad, instead of laying off flight crews, the airline put them to work loading bags, taking tickets – anything to keep them working. The policy has paid off in terms of company loyalty and individual productivity.

The crash of 191 had both a financial and a psychological effect on Delta. The former was negligible. On Monday, August 5, Delta's stock closed at 49 1/2, off 7/8. The effect on the "Delta family" was considerably more profound. The reaction of one employee was typical: "I've been a reservationist for many years," she confided to a psychiatrist. "I thought flying Delta was invincible. I've always told customers I didn't think we'd ever crash."

Jim Ewings's reaction was similar. He was at his North Atlanta home on August 2. Taking a day off, he had just finished mowing the lawn and was watching the evening news on PBS when, at 7:10 p.m. Eastern Time, the phone rang. "It's Flight Control," he told his wife. "They've got something bad. I can feel it in my guts." From the kitchen, she responded, "Jim, you say that every time the phone rings." This time, the intuition was right.

"What do we have here?" he asked the supervisor at Delta's Hartsfield International headquarters. "Do we have survivability?" "Jim, I don't think so. There was a big fireball and an explosion." "What kind of plane?" "An L1011," came the reply. "It can't be an L1011!" shot back the incredulous executive. "They just don't crash. They're crashproof."

The record almost backs him up. Since the widebody's introduction in 1972, there had been only two crashes of the Lockheed craft. On December 29, 1972, an Eastern TriStar on approach to Miami flew into the Everglades. Seventy-six of the 175 people on board survived. The accident was the basis for the book, *The Ghost of Flight 401*. On August 19, 1980, a Saudi Arabian Airlines L1011 enroute to Jeddah made an emergency landing at Riyadh after an in-flight fire traced to a cargo bin. The airplane landed safely, pulled off on a taxiway, and burned. All on board perished.   **91**

These episodes aside, pilot and industry praise for the TriStar have been virtually universal. A 1982 issue of *OAG/Frequent Flyer* magazine termed the plane "one of the cleanest, quietest, most technologically advanced aircraft ever produced. It also is one of the safest aircraft flying today." The highly respected British aerospace weekly *Flight International* labeled the craft "the best American widebody," adding, "the Lockheed TriStar's popular reputation as a very safe aircraft is endorsed by the record." Ironically, the L10 lost an estimated $2.5 billion for Lockheed. In the marketplace, if not the safety column, it was beaten out by another trijet: the DC-10.

Hanging up the phone, Ewing rushed to his closet, donned a suit, and jumped in his son's 280Z. He covered the distance between North Atlanta and Hartsfield, on the south end of town, in half an hour. On the way, he listened to a tape of classical organ music, steeling himself for the ordeal ahead.

He pulled up to the guard gate at Delta headquarters at 8 p.m. Eastern Time. In Dallas, it was 7:00. The helicopter carrying Baby X was just landing at Parkland. Ewing began his work as the last of the living was evacuated from the scene of the still-smoldering jet.

The company's standard operating plan was already in effect. Telephone technicians in Fort Lauderdale, Dallas, and Los Angeles had established special lines to the Delta Command Center in Atlanta. Voice speakers crackled, phones rang, and television monitors cast a flickering pale blue light across the scene. From the hubbub, Ewing gathered the basics: the flight number, origin, destination, number of passengers, and number of crew. In a hurriedly prepared initial release, he said that there appeared to be no survivors. As he walked across the parking lot to face assembled television cameras with the company's first official statement, he prayed. "Lord, I need help. Bad. I want to say the right thing, and I want to say it the right way." Later, he reflected on his feelings that evening: "We let people down. You see, we have a responsibility to the passengers. We may not have any blame coming out of this, the probable cause. But in our minds, we let somebody down. We have a responsibility to get a passenger from Point A to Point B in safety and comfort. We have a contract with them—a moral contract."

Coming from most public relations people, it would sound self-serving. From Ewing, his piercing eyes framed by spare wire-rims, his voice choked by obvious emotion, the impression is of uncut sincerity.

As the evening raced on, Delta drew in people from all over its route structure to deal with the most immediate mandate: notifying the families. Eighty-six marketing representatives were initially contacted. They were sent to Florida, California, and Texas. It soon became apparent that families weren't confined to origin and destination; they were spread across the country. District directors and passenger service agents were called in. About 1:30 a.m. Eastern Time, the red-eyed, uniformed employees started to make "the bad calls." In person, Delta representatives started knocking on doors, delivering the news. Positive identifications were still lacking on most victims, and the list of survivors had just been compiled. Delta just wanted the families to know they were there. Most families took the airline up on its offer of carte blanche assistance. Some, like the Clarks in Minnesota, couldn't initially be located.

The crash has left emotional scars on a proud airline, some of them deep. More than one Delta representative who dealt with the victim's families says the crash was like a death in their family. Are these simply examples of corporate come-on, well-rehearsed "sentiment" played back for maximum PR benefit?

In the wake of 191, the sentiment rang true. Grief lays bare the most basic emotions. Artifice is not easily achieved when nerve endings are raw and eyes are red. Grief strips off job titles, what Sartre calls one's "facticity," and reveals the human being. Delta people did grieve – for the dead and those left behind, for their airline, their family.

THE HUMAN FACTOR

Fifty-seven-year-old Edward Michael Connors was unmistakably an airline captain. If the easy smile and assured manner weren't tipoffs, the eyes were. They bore the indelible mark of a pilot of the line: crow's-feet. The tiny spiderweb creases are as much a sign of a pilot's prowess as his wings—maybe more, for wings don't betray the thousands of hours spent hunched over a dimly lit instrument panel or squinting against the glare of a naked sun.

Twenty-nine thousand, three hundred hours of Ted Connors's life had been spent flying airplanes. He was the type of guy featured in airline ads when they still stressed competence over aircraft color schemes. Airmen who knew him said he was a by-the-book pilot who "always tried to stay ahead of the airplane." Others who flew with Connors labeled him meticulous and cautious. One copilot cited a flight from Los Angeles in which Connors decided to return to the airport rather than continue the trip when a faulty fuel gauge was discovered. Another remembered an instance in which Connors used "excessive" caution to fly around a thunderstorm while other flights followed more direct routes. As a result, his plane was fifteen minutes late.

For even the most cautious of pilots, flying has its moments. Connors's came in May 1969. En route from New York to Miami, his 727 was hijacked by a trio of armed thugs demanding to fly to Havana. As added inducement to follow their orders, one of them held a knife to the throat of a flight attendant. Ted Connors's interest in the woman's welfare went beyond the responsibility bestowed by the four stripes on his sleeves. She was his wife.

Under intense professional and personal pressure, Connors flew by the book and landed in Cuba. The terrorists got off. He delivered his command safely to Miami. The man was a consummate pro.

Colleagues called forty-three-year-old first officer Rudolph Przydzial Price, Jr., a "quiet" man, "very stable and an above-average" pilot. His logbook recorded 6,500 hours. Yet he knew the L1011 perhaps more intimately than any pilot in the airline. In 1977 Rudy Price was selected to help rewrite Delta's operating manual for the TriStar. After the two-year effort he told a coworker, "Jets are not forgiving. They're marvelous machines, but they don't forgive mistakes. Still, of all of 'em, the L1011 is the most forgiving."

One coworker labeled him "an airman's airman." The moniker was earned in Southeast Asia. For a while, the South China Sea was Price's home, Indochina his office. There he learned many things, among them the visceral niceties of landing a fighter on a rolling, heaving deck in the middle of the night. A devoted Roman Catholic, he spent much of his free time ministering to a prison outreach program in Georgia. With family, flying, and charity work, friends say that he didn't have a lot of time for other pursuits, with one notable exception. That exception was the weather. Rudy Price was an amateur meteorologist.

Neither Connors nor Price was a "cowboy," a species of pilot not entirely unknown to commercial aviation. Evidence is persuasive that neither knew the true nature of what lay off the end of runway 17L. If they had, past performance predicts that neither would have attempted penetration. However unfounded, the shadowy spectre of pilot error will probably forever haunt Delta 191. It lurks in legal briefs and whispered conversations. Evidence never fully exorcises suspicion, nor logic innuendo.

The death of 191 may not have been due to pilot error, but the fact is that man remains the weakest link in the safety equation. Jim Burnett, chairman of the National Transportation Safety Board, labeled pilot performance "one of the last frontiers in aviation safety," adding, "We have been more successful in dealing with problems that have to do with hardware than we have in dealing with problems that have to do with humans."

Human factors played a pivotal role in the 1971 crash of a prop-jet Convair at the small New England city of New Haven. According to the accident report, the pilot was behind schedule, having just made three fog bound missed approaches at New London, before landing there on the fourth try. At New Haven, his next stop, the pilot decided to try another approach, again to a fog shrouded runway. Despite advisories by his copilot that the airplane had gone below Minimum Descent Altitude, the fatal approach continued. The plane plunged into a row of beach cottages.

The crew of perhaps the most publicized crash in modern commercial history, Air Florida Flight 90, did a lot of things wrong, according to the NTSB, like not aborting a doomed takeoff. It was a matter of judgment. But what led to the fatal decision to milk the runway at Washington National of virtually every available foot before mushing into the wintry skies in pathetic imitation of a climb? What pride, passions, and human proclivities lie behind the facile phrase "pilot error"? What is "the real why"?

THE HUMAN FACTOR

Michael J. Pangia is the former chief of the FAA's Litigation Division: "Unless we begin to answer that question and apply the resulting intelligence to increase self-awareness of the judgment-making process, we can expect the percentage of accidents attributable to 'human error' to remain high." Panagia wrote those words during a remarkable twenty-six-month hiatus, a period free of major air crashes in the United States. "Palm 90" (the reference to the Air Florida 737 by controllers at National) ended the streak when it plunged into the Potomac, killing seventy-four of the seventy-nine people on board as well as four motorists who were unlucky enough to be on the 14th Street Bridge at the wrong time.

Research by the International Air Transport Association indicates that some 70 percent of takeoff and landing accidents involve human error. Yet, until very recently, there has been a fundamental flaw in the way aircraft accident investigation has been approached. Dr. A. Diehl, a former senior safety investigator with the NTSB's Human Factors Division, put it this way: "By investigating only for 'probable cause,' the tendency is to examine wreckage for evidence of mechanical problems. When none are found, the investigator concludes that the crew was at fault and some type of generic label is invoked such as 'failed to see and avoid,' 'improper use of controls,' or 'failed to arrest descent at decision height.' Unfortunately, all too often, precious little effort is made to ascertain *why* the pilot 'erred' " (author's emphasis).

James W. Danaher is past director of the NTSB's Bureau of Technology. When he began his career with the safety board in 1970, it was as chief of human factors. None of his team was formally trained in the behavioral sciences. Danaher says Human Factors "at that time was not really strongly oriented toward the underlying why of human performance which led to accidents." Human Factors' investigators "were more concerned with the survival aspects" of crashes, the human involvement in the consequences of an accident. Danaher remembers grimly that when he first joined NTSB, Human Factors people "were known as 'the fingers and toes' boys because they gathered up the pieces, arranged the autopsies, and duly recorded the injuries."

Danaher realized that there had to be a new focus. So did his boss, the legendary aviation safety pioneer C. O. Miller. Danaher recalls, "He really said he'd **97** like to see us get at the underlying whys of accident causation." Thus began a crusade of sorts within the bureaucracy. The NTSB took a tentative yet significant step in 1980 during its investigation of a Downeast Airlines commuter crash. In efforts to probe the dynamics of "the real why," the board examined the crew's physiological and psychological conditions just prior to the crash, which claimed seventeen lives.

The accident report indicates that the captain was not an assertive person and was subject to constant company pressure. He remained with the carrier while fellow pilots departed in droves. He also showed classic signs of stress: loss of appetite, exhaustion, breathing difficulties. The NTSB noted that that level of stress, over an extended period of time, could cause depression and chronic fatigue.

On the evening of May 30, 1979, during poor weather, the DHC-6 Twin Otter was literally flown into the ground. This nonassertive captain, a seventeen-year veteran and Downeast's chief pilot, was judged by those who flew with him to be a good airman. Still, he worked for a company president who allegedly demanded that pilots make repeated instrument approaches and "get lower" during bad weather. To top that, the NTSB's report says the president allegedly ridiculed pilots in front of their peers, suggesting that those who were unable to land when others had were less skilled, even cowards. An overbearing boss and a competent yet complacent chief pilot: were those "the real whys"? The NTSB says as much. The report was a real breakthrough, one in which logic finally slew jargon:

> "Although the safety board was unable to determine conclusively the reason(s) for the flight crew's deviation from standard instrument approach procedures, it is believed that inordinate management pressures, the first officer's marginal instrument proficiency, the captain's inadequate supervision of the flight, inadequate crew training and procedures and the captain's chronic fatigue were all factors in the accident."

This new approach received another boost in March 1982 with the confirmation of Burnett as chairman. Even though the previous few years had been lean ones for the safety board, Burnett said that positions would be created to staff a new Human Performance Division. The team that resulted from Burnett's move is like none other at NTSB. Says Danaher, "We wanted to take someone with formal training in the behavioral sciences and try to make them investigators rather than taking pilots and investigators and trying to teach them psychology." Some old-guard staffers were skeptical about the shift in emphasis. But skeptical or not, the psychologists are already making their presence felt.

A behavioral profile is proving to be an essential tool in crash investigation. In addition to the usual questions about what the crew ate and drank and how much sleep they got, the profile probes assertiveness, cooperation, decision-making characteristics, and other hard-to-quantify factors. A couple of the questions: "Does/did he/she have any personal financial or family problems?" and "Has anyone close to him/her been seriously ill or just died?"

The difficulty, contends Jim Danaher, is in relating what is culled from a behavioral profile to a pilot's performance at a specific point in time: "It's a whole constellation of facts, conditions, and circumstances which – taken collectively – one can intuitively say really have a high probability of influencing performance adversely. But we're still talking *probabilities*." Forging a compelling link between cause and effect is the real challenge. When do the questions stop being astute and become merely absurd? It's a topic much on the mind of the Air Line Pilots Association.

"Some of the areas they're going into are just not amenable to any scientific approach to accident investigation," says ALPA official Harold Marthinsen. "There's no way you can tie in the fact that somebody has financial problems to an accident. I mean, we all have financial problems. We're a little bit cautious about where they're going in this so-called 'psychological autopsy' business."

Instead of "psychological autopsies," ALPA wants the NTSB's Human Performance team to concentrate more on what Marthinsen calls the "human engineering aspects of accident investigation," such as cockpit layout and instrument readability.

Perhaps the pilot's union is concerned where the whole psychological approach could lead. Little is known of Soviet accident investigation. Aeroflot doesn't send its reports to the International Civil Aviation Organization in Montreal. In part, it's a case of embarrassment. IL-62s, TU-144s, and TU-154s are not put together very well. Even though the West is not privy to Soviet investigations, evidence indicates that psychologists play an important part in the day-to-day operations of the world's largest airline.

Dr. Stanley R. Mohler is the former chief of the FAA's Aeromedical Applications Division. During a thaw in Soviet-American relations in the mid-1970s, he viewed firsthand Aeroflot's approach to aviation medicine, one that has a definite behaviorist bent. Mohler says that a crewmember is assigned a specific Aeroflot doctor and that "the physician is required to periodically visit the family of each crewmember and assist with *any medical-social problems that could result in mental distraction or other psychological or emotional difficulties*" (author's emphasis).

In addition to Big Brotherly home visits, crewmembers are given preflight exams prior to the initial departure of each trip. As of the mid-1970s, some ten million preflight exams were conducted annually. Permission to fly was denied in about nine thousand cases.

Is the personally invasive Soviet approach the way to go? Aeroflot's safety record is horrendous. How much worse it might be without the exams, no one knows. What about other forms of psychological exams, such as those practiced in the West? The military and many airlines require personality profiles of their prospective pilots. Still, human error accidents proliferate. Mere profiles are not the answer.

C. I. Barron was an adjunct professor of aviation physiology at UCLA when he wrote, "Psychological testing is all too brief and inadequate in civil aviation and not entirely relevant in military exams. The Air Traffic Controller is given more consideration in this area than the airman."

Even comprehensive psychological tests are lacking unless they spark self-

99

awareness. The past assumption that a person either possesses good judgment or doesn't is suspect. Positive behavior modifications have been accomplished in fields ranging from child psychology to corporate management. Former FAA official Pangia asks, "Can the aviation population afford to consider itself impervious to positive change in this regard?"

At first glance, simulators seem to infuse the right stuff. They are extraordinarily sophisticated and can duplicate gut-wrenching problems without ever leaving the ground. The newer flying machines are better, too. Cockpits are ergonomically designed with human engineering as a guiding philosophy. In ships like the 767 and A310, pilots are less likely to make errors caused by the machine's not fitting the person.

Still, simulations, state-of-the-art instrumentation, and ergonomics do little to change the way one perceives the world. Many human error accidents aren't caused by lack of information available to the pilot or the placement of critical controls. They are born in the human mind, in the very subjective way a pilot filters data through a labyrinth of physical and psychological needs. In short, the grey-templed, lantern-jawed guy up front can be distressingly like you and me.

The human mind is a subtle thing. And while bureaucracy is finally beginning to unlock its workings, there are some areas many still consider too delicate or far-fetched to probe.

In the spring of 1977, the crew of Southern Airways 242, on a flight from Huntsville, Alabama, to Atlanta, tried to shoot the gap between two monstrous thunderheads. What appeared to be a path to safety on the radar screen was really an unholy gauntlet of hail. The compressor blades of the DC-9's JT-8D engines stalled in the deluge, causing the power plants to melt. Flight 242 became a glider, one with the flying characteristics of a falling safe.

Unable to restart the engines or make it to a nearby airport, Captain Bill McKenzie tells copilot Lyman Keele, "Like we are. I'm picking out a clear field."

Keele, who is actually flying the plane, says, "Bill, you've got to find me a highway."

McKenzie: "Let's take the next open field."

Keele: "No!"

McKenzie: "See a highway over—no cars."

Keele: "Right there, is that straight?"

McKenzie: "No."

Keele: "We'll have to take it."

McKenzie radios controllers, "We're putting it down on a highway—we're down to nothing."

Keele (to McKenzie): "Flaps."

McKenzie: "They're at 50 (degrees)."

Keele: "Oh–Bill, I hope we can do it."

There is a car on the road. Keele tells McKenzie: "I've got, I got it. I'm going to land right over that guy."

McKenzie: "There's a car ahead."

Keele: "I've got it, Bill. I've got it now. I got it."

McKenzie: "Okay."

McKenzie: "Don't stall it."

Keele: "I gotta bug [1.3 of stall speed]. We're gonna do it right here."

Wheels touch. The plane is moving at 130 knots. It bounces.

Out of a cacophanous hell of tearing metal punctuated by explosions comes a tortured human sound from the cockpit, a barely intelligible cry of frustration. Seventy-one people died that day on the main thoroughfare of a tiny Georgia hamlet with the improbable name of New Hope. After the official investigation was over, an intriguing theory was brought to light involving "biometeorology – the study of the relationship between weather and living organisms. Dr. E. Stanton Maxey, a Florida biophysicist, surgeon, and qualified flight instructor, expounded the notion that weather can have a profound, often disastrous effect on judgment. The theory is called the Caged Brain Syndrome.

In 1976 Maxey delivered his blockbuster paper to a meeting of the Civil Aviation Medical Association. He chronicled a number of fatal crashes during the 1970s and said, "In each case – and many, many smaller ones could be gathered from the accident records – the pilots were traversing inclement weather. Low-frequency magnetic waves are known to directly affect brain functions in some persons. I submit that these pilots may have been such persons. I further submit that their brains may have been caged by the then-extant magnetic component of the weather they so disastrously failed to traverse. And I strongly suspect that such accidents will cease only after aviation's medical fraternity recognizes these phenomena and effects application of remedial devices."

A kook? A "mad scientist" indulging in academic folly? Not at all. In 1969 the Swedish government worked out a very specific correlation between accidents and magnetic storms. The astonishing conclusions became a military secret.

When an airplane crashes, public attention is focused on the quick fix. New hardware is easy to get a handle on; it translates readily into consumer causes and budget proposals. While hardware can be vital – as especially in the case of Delta 191 – there are times when it's not enough, times when we must move beyond mere symptoms and attack the causes of the disease, "the real why."

SHEAR IGNORANCE

The most dramatic wind shear accident of all never happened.

Two years and a day before 191 crashed, a blue and white Boeing 707 descended from the threatening skies over rural Maryland. The eight tires of the main undercarriage echoed a sharp, quick bark as they met macadam. Touchdown was at approximately 14:04 Eastern Daylight Time. The pilot reversed the thrust of his four powerful Pratt & Whitney engines and taxied the craft toward the ramp to unload his passengers.

Some six and a half minutes after landing, the sky fell. At 14:10:45, a northwesterly wind gust upwards of 130 knots was recorded by instruments on the field. A short time later, the anemometer was almost becalmed: 2 knots of wind, no more. At 14:13:40, another burst buffeted the gauge: 87 knots, from the southeast.

The phenomenon was a wind shear, one of extraordinary power. The plane it missed by mere minutes bore another kind of power—mighty, yet decidedly mortal. Historians will not find that 707—Air Force One—on the list of twenty-seven aircraft felled in the United States by low-level wind shear since 1964. Nor will they find Ronald Reagan's name among the 628 slain. But it was close.

Wind shear is nothing new. An artist depicted what is probably one of the earliest recorded examples in a 1671 English journal. The phenomenon has probably been knocking planes from the sky for decades. The crashes were most often pinned on "pilot error." Only with the coming of the 1970s—and pioneering work by Dr. Ted Fujita of the University of Chicago—did we begin to understand the true nature of the beast.

Wind shear itself is not necessarily dangerous. It's an accepted fact of life aloft and exists at virtually all altitudes. Wherever there is a divergent flow of air, there is a shear. Airliners fly through them every day. Most of the time they go unnoticed. At the cruising altitude of most commercial jets (33,000 to 41,000 feet) and normal speeds (Mach .82 or so), shears pose virtually no threat. It's at lower levels and slower speeds that they begin to affect aircraft performance. To realize why, it is critical to understand "lift," the foundation of all aeronautical law and prophecy.

Initially, people believed that in order for a machine to fly, its wings had to flap like a bird's. With the invention of the glider by Sir George Cayley in 1804, we learned differently. Humankind first ascended on fixed, not flexed, wings. This was made possible by a rule of physics called Bernoulli's Theorem. The faster the air moves, the less internal pressure it has. Early experimenters discovered that they could coax far more lift from a wing whose upper surface was curved. The air passing over the curved upper surface has to travel farther and faster than the air flowing beneath. This creates a pressure imbalance. The airfoil is actually sucked up into the low-pressure area while being pushed up by higher pressure underneath. For the theory to work, air must move continuously over the wing from front (the leading edge) to rear (the trailing edge) at sufficient speed.

The rate at which a plane moves through a stream of air is called the Indicated Air Speed, or IAS. This is a decidedly different notion from ground speed. Some headwinds have proven so strong that aircraft have actually flown backwards. A negative ground speed and a positive airspeed are extremely rare, although entirely possible. As long as air moves across the wing at speeds sufficient to produce lift, the craft will fly.

Conversely, very strong tailwinds can produce anemic airspeed (and thus insufficient lift) while yielding gangbuster ground speed. The craft moves rapidly across the earth, but it can also close quickly with it. Put simply, airplanes are creatures of the air, and the air is a dimension with its own rules: immutable, subtle, and unforgiving.

When Dr. Fujita began his research into wind shear, a new term was coined: "downburst." It is a localized, intense downdraft of wind whose vertical currents exceed 12 feet per second (720 feet per minute) at 300 feet above the surface. When a downburst is 2½ miles across or less it is called a "microburst," the most deadly manifestation of wind shear. As this tremendous vertical blast hits the ground, it rushes horizontally in all directions, sometimes as fast as 168 mph. At the same time, it can curl up and in, producing a roiling, churning ricochet that resembles a tornado lying on its side. This is the vortex curl, the last and perhaps most savage effect of the burst.

In the southern and eastern parts of the United States, microbursts are most often spawned by thunderstorms. In the west, they can be the product of more benign-appearing clouds. In either case, they are not to be trifled with.

"The problem with a microburst is pretty simple," says Dr. John McCarthy of the National Center for Atmospheric Research (NCAR). "When you enter one, you

104

often get a headwind increase as you fly through this initial outflow on one side. That may be misleading to the pilot, because his performance [airspeed] is increasing. It can lull a pilot into the belief that there is really no serious problem. Just a few seconds later, the headwind decays as he flys into the downdraft. Finally, on the backside of the microburst, you get a strong increase in the tailwind component. The bottom line is that the aircraft is in a serious performance loss situation. Depending on how it's flown and the intensity of the microburst, that's big trouble."

Through a series of studies, scientists have determined that when a typical microburst first hits the ground, it sparks a shear of some 24 knots. This does not necessarily pose a serious problem. However, in the next three to seven minutes the shear intensifies, reaching, on average, 47 knots. Such a shear on takeoff or landing is a potential killer. The crash of Pan American Flight 759 in Kenner, Louisiana, dramatically illustrates the point. Experts have estimated that the shear that hit the fully loaded 727 was a fatally "average" 47 knots. The July 9, 1982 crash killed 153 people.

Air Traffic Control warned the crew of Flight 759 about wind shear that day. The Low Level Wind Shear Alert System (LLWSAS) had just gone off in the tower when New Orleans Ground Control broadcast: "We have, ah, low level wind shear alerts all quadrants. Appears the frontal passing overhead right now. We're right in the middle of everything."

Flight 759 is still on the ground preparing for takeoff. On hearing the warning, an unidentified member of the cockpit crew says something unintelligible. A second later, the captain tells the copilot, who will actually make the takeoff: "Let your speed build up on takeoff." Some investigators have interpreted this to mean that the crewmembers were fully aware of the shear and wanted to give themselves an extra margin of speed with which to weather any expected loss of lift.

At 15:05:20, the captain picks up the public address mike and tells a cabin full of expectant passengers: "Ah, good afternoon, ladies and gentlemen. We would like to welcome our New Orleans passengers aboard the–the continuation of Flight 759 to Las Vegas and San Diego. We'll be ready for takeoff momentarily. We'd ask you to please ensure that your seat belts are all buckled up. We'll be cruising at **105** 31,000 feet to Las Vegas. Estimated flying time is three hours and ten minutes. After takeoff we'll be maneuvering around, circumnavigating some, ah, some little thunder-showers out there, so we would like to ask you folks to please remain in your seats. We thank you. Flight attendant, please secure the cabin."

Unlike Delta 191, the crew appears to have been aware of both thunder-storms and shear. They decided to give it a go, anyway. Investigators believe that in an effort to determine how to avoid the worst of the stuff, the crew was looking either directly at the weather off the end of Moisant International Airport's Runway 10 or at their radar scope, when, at 15:07:44, the copilot asked the captain: "Right turn or left turn when we get out of here?"

15:07:48 – CAPTAIN: "A little north [to the left]."

15:07:50 – COPILOT: "We're cleared for takeoff."

15:07:52 – CAPTAIN: "I would suggest–"

15:07:52 – FLIGHT ENGINEER: "Looking good."

15:07:53 – CAPTAIN: "–a slight turn over to the left."

15:07:56 – COPILOT: "Okay."

15:07:56 – FLIGHT ENGINEER: "Takeoff checks all done."

15:07:59 – COPILOT: "Takeoff thrust."

The die is cast, but the house has weighted the cubes. Clipper 759 has precisely one minute and six seconds of life left. Today there will be no champagne celebrations on the way to Las Vegas, not even in First Class. For all souls on board there will be only momentary horror, half a beat short of full recognition. Then, there will be nothing:

15:08:04 – COPILOT: "Need the wipers."

15:08:06 – The sound of windscreen wipers begins as rain begins its impact. The noise continues till the end of the tape.

15:08:16 – A thump similar to a bump on the runway. The 727 is barreling toward takeoff speed.

15:08:16 – UNIDENTIFIED CREWMEMBER: "Eighty knots."

15:08:27 – There is a click in the cockpit. The tempo from the wipers increases. It's a tattoo of death.

15:08:28 – A final bump from the runway. The next sound transmitted from earth to airplane will be of an altogether different quality.

15:08:33 – CAPTAIN: "Vee R" (the speed at which the nose of the plane comes off the ground, or "rotates").

15:08:41 – CAPTAIN: "Positive climb."

15:08:42 – COPILOT: "Gear up."

15:08:43 – CAPTAIN: "Vee two" (a climb reference speed).

15:08:45 – CAPTAIN: "Come on back. You're sinking, Don. Come on back."

15:08:48 – The sound of the nose gear settling into place is heard above the noise of the rain.

15:08:51 – ATC LOCAL CONTROL: "Clipper 759 contact departure [controller on frequency] one two seven point six. So long."

The words possess a chilling, if unintentional, double meaning. Clipper is falling:

15:08:57 – The sound of the Ground Proximity Warning System is sepulcher, synthetic: "Whoop whoop – pull up! Whoop –"

15:09:00 – The sound of the first impact is recorded on the cockpit voice recorder as metal and treetop meet.

15:09:02 – From somewhere in the cockpit there is what the NTSB calls a "nonpertinent word." One can only imagine.

15:09:04 – Another impact.

15:09:05 – There is a final sound. The short flight of Clipper 759 is over.

The fatal wind that felled 759 was "average." The one that killed Delta 191 was anything but. The shear of August 2 was – at flight level – a 72-knot creature, compounded by hellacious up- and downdrafts created by vortex curls. The crash of 191 taught investigators things they never knew about the dynamics of a microburst. In terms of accident investigation, the date derived from the Digital Flight Data Recorder (DFDR) of N726DA proved to be a gold mine. The ore was refined through a process of **107** sophisticated simulation, and that taught them even more.

The DFDR and its inferior counterpart, the FDR (Flight Data Recorder), are the famed "black boxes." Actually they, along with the cockpit voice recorder, are painted bright orange for quick identification. To boost their chances of surviving a crash, the FAA mandates that they be located "as far aft as practicable." The metal alloy casings in which they are housed are extraordinarily tough. They must withstand 1,000-G drops right side up, on the side, and on end. In addition, repeated shots with a high-tensile weight are applied, as well as 5,000 pounds of crushing pressure for five minutes. Finally, 50 percent of the shell is blasted with a scorching 2,000-degree flame.

Before black boxes, aircraft accident investigation was like "operating with your head in a sack," says Bob Rudich, former chief of the NTSB's Audio Laboratory in Washington. In his lab, the first CVR tapes were read out and analyzed.

Early accident investigators gleaned information largely by piecing together giant jigsaw puzzles. Instruments, control surfaces (rudders, elevators, and ailerons), engines, and airframes were meticulously studied in engineering postmortems. The procedure is still used. But, taken alone, the method left a lot of questions unanswered. The first investigators were aviation archaeologists who attempted to draw meaning from piles of aluminum rubble. The FDR and CVR changed that. With their advent, investigators were able to sketch what happened in the final crucial moments of flight. The phrase "probable cause" became more credible and answers to the question "Why?" a bit less elusive.

The FDR, a giant stride when it was introduced in the late 1950s, is now woefully obsolete. Yet it is still used on a large percentage of older commercial jets. It documents only four performance factors: magnetic heading, Indicated Air Speed, vertical acceleration (G's), and pressure altitude. A fifth element, radio transmission time, is also noted. It can be synchronized with the magnetic tape recording from the CVR.

FDR data is roughly etched on metal foil by a series of sharp styli. The harsh metallic portrait is incomplete. Like a black and white photo of an old master painting, it lacks color and nuance. A product of 1950s technology, the FDR has now been eclipsed by the DFDR.

Pan Am 759, a Boeing 727, was equipped with the archaic metal stylus recorders. The information it yielded about wind shear was incomplete. Until the crash of 191, which was equipped with a multiparameter DFDR, investigators had only a grainy, blurred snapshot of a microburst. Now they have a hologram.

Jeffrey Gorney is an aerospace engineer with NTSB: "Of the information we took off the flight recorders from Delta 191 – as far as all past wind shear accident studies – this has been the most bountiful and highest quality data." Gorney says "there ain't no way in hell" that accurate wind profiles could have been culled from the limited information provided by the FDRs aboard Pan Am 759 and Eastern Airlines Flight 66, another victim of wind shear.

"In the other wind shear accidents," says Gorney, "we couldn't really identify what was clearly any vortex action, up- and downdrafts in the wind shear itself. . . . The fact is that the aircraft [191] not only traversed a wind shear in the horizontal plane but at the same time went through a series of very severe up- and downdrafts." The young NTSB staffer says the TriStar was "also hit by some very severe lateral gusts from the right as it approached the airport. All these occurred within a matter of seconds. You really had a three-pronged attack here, in all the axes. He [copilot Rudy Price] took a 20-knot airspeed loss in one second. Within a couple of seconds of that, he was hit by a severe updraft." In effect, Gorney describes a heaving, rolling, bucking bronco in the guise of a 324,821-pound airplane.

After the NTSB hearing, the Boeing Commercial Airplane Company and United Airlines took the data from the DFDR, which had been refined into a wind model by the National Aeronautics and Space Administration, and ran it through sophisticated, ground-based aircraft simulators.

Pilots are taught to stay away from areas of known wind shear. If they find themselves in one, there is a very specific escape technique, one that runs contrary to everything they have learned since they started flying. First, we must recognize that stalling an airplane on takeoff or landing is the worst thing that can happen. A stall occurs when the air no longer moves across the top surface of the wing at sufficient speeds to produce lift. The smooth flow of air becomes a turbulent, roiling cauldron, and the vacuum effect of the airfoil is destroyed. Lift dies, and so does the airplane.

Stall occurs when Indicated Air Speed drops below a given point. The value depends on a number of variables: the type of aircraft, its weight, the temperature, the altitude, and other factors. Stall speed is carefully calculated before each flight. The speed of an aircraft can be controlled in two ways: by using power levers (throttles) and the control column (the yoke). Advance the levers and the plane moves faster. Pitch the nose forward and you get the same effect. An incipient stall is countered by pushing the nose down. The technique is fast and effective.

Conversely, there is no quicker way to precipitate a stall than to yank back on the yoke. As the nose pitches up, airspeed plummets. In the cockpit of modern jetliners, stall is foreshadowed by stickshaker. Just before stall is reached, the yoke begins to shake in a pronounced, vibratory rattle. The warning is unmistakable: tactile, visual, and auditory. At high altitudes, the pilot can afford to shed some height by pushing forward on the control column. Closer to the ground, there is precious little pad between airplane and earth. To squelch a stall, the pilot eases off stickshaker just a scoch. What he doesn't do is pull back on the yoke.

Enter wind shear. Virtually all such accidents occur on takeoff or landing, when the aircraft is close to the ground. When a pilot sees the bottom fall out of the airspeed, his natural reaction is to push forward on the power levers and the yoke. The aim is to recover lost airspeed. However, since the plane is already losing altitude as a result of the shear, a nose-down attitude just accelerates the fall. The pilot faces a dilemma. Does he recover air speed, only to plow into the ground, or does he risk a deadly stall by hauling back on the column?

Recovery techniques taught in the wake of the crash of Eastern Flight 66 tell pilots to ram the throttles all the way to the firewall if necessary and pull the nose up, all the way to stickshaker, if they have to. It can work, but the technique goes against every ingrained reaction with which the pilot grew up.

Just how well the technique can work is illustrated by a wind shear encounter that never made the headlines. Almost six years before 191 went down, Eastern Airlines Flight 693, a Boeing 727 carrying seventy-one passengers and a crew of six, came within 375 feet of crashing just short of Runway 27L at Atlanta's busy Hartsfield International Airport. As with Eastern 66, Pan Am 759, and Delta 191, the first officer (copilot) was flying the plane.

It was hot on the afternoon of August 22, 1979. Locally heavy rain showers dotted the area. For Flight 693, the trip from Indianapolis had been routine until it started to make an instrument approach to 27L. At 15:10 the local controller cleared 693 to land, adding, "The winds are calm and keep your speed up as long as possible on final, sir. You'll break out of that rain shower in about three miles, and there is rain down the middle of Runway 27 Left right now."

The captain of 693 knew there was rain ahead. He monitored the communications between the two flights preceding him on approach, a Delta L1011 and a Delta 727. There was no word of anything except the shower.

As 693 continued down the approach path, it began to encounter light rain and turbulence combined with a bit of airspeed fluctuation—nothing out of the ordinary. About a thousand feet above ground level, rain and turbulence increased. The tempo of the precipitation picked up, becoming "heavy." At the same time, the first intimations of wind shear revealed themselves. The Indicated Air Speed shed 15 knots, dropping from 135 to 120. Then it ballooned by 20 knots as the 727 entered the front of the microburst. Seconds later, the bottom dropped out: 108. The 727 began to fall, first at 1,000 feet per minute, then 1,500. Finally it plummeted at a gut-wrenching 2,000 feet per minute. Flight 693 was rapidly running out of air.

At first the copilot pulled the nose up 10 degrees and called for takeoff power. Nothing. Then he hauled back another 5 degrees and rammed the power levers all the way to their forward stops. Around 500 feet, the stickshaker went off. At almost the same instant the Ground Proximity Warning System triggered: "Whoop, whoop—pull up!" Afraid of stalling, the copilot eased off the stickshaker, dropping the nose from 15 to 12 degrees. By now Flight 693 was closing with the ground at 2,200 feet per minute. If something didn't work soon—

It did. At 375 feet above the earth, the 727 flew out of the precipitation, right wing down, and began to climb toward the heavens. The captain radioed the local controller: "There's quite a bit of rain—a wind shear out here. I don't see how anybody could make an approach to the left one (Runway 27L)."

Disaster was averted by seconds. The affair was labeled an "incident." In its report the NTSB said in effect that Flight 693 flew out of the shear because of a combination of luck and skill:

> The performance data disclosed that two factors combined to prevent the wind shear encounter from creating an accident. The first was the variation of the downdraft pattern from the classic configuration normally present in this type of phenomenon. Between the OM (Outer Marker to Runway 27L) and the establishment of the missed approach climb, the winds which influenced the aircraft were, sequentially, as follows: headwind, a combination of headwind downdraft, downdraft and headwind. Instead of encountering the downwind portion of the outflow pattern after the downdraft was traversed, Flight 693 encountered a substantial headwind. This, in effect, immediately increased the aircraft's climb capability, *and therefore increased its ability to attain a positive vertical speed and execute the missed approach* [author's emphasis].
>
> The second factor which enabled the flight to traverse the wind shear was the fact that, except for the momentary overcorrection in response to the stall warning, the first officer attempted to maneuver his aircraft in accordance with the procedures that he had seen demonstrated during wind shear training in the flight simulator. When he recognized the onset of this particular shear, he did not try to reestablish the landing approach: takeoff thrust was applied; the aircraft was rotated to pitch nagle, which activated the stickshaker; then the nose was lowered until the stickshaker stopped, and the aircraft's nose was raised again. Finally, the pilots applied the total thrust available [by pushing the power levers to their stops] even though that meant exceeding engine limitations. Although the performance calculations indicated that recovery did not take place until the headwind component was entered, the flightcrew's tactics delayed the aircraft's descent and helped keep it airborne until the downburst area had been traversed.

The crew of 693 didn't fall into the trap of "chasing airspeed." The copilot refused to trade precious altitude for speed, even though he was hovering on the edge of a stall. But how about Delta 191? It is true that the crew had no idea what they were getting into. But once there, did they use proper recovery techniques?

The analysis done by NASA for the NTSB at the space agency's Ames Research Center indicated, in theory, that 191 could have successfully flown through the monster off the end of 17L. The report sparked a storm of controversy. The implication was clear: Connors and Price might not have erred in flying *into* the thing, but they seem to have botched the attempt to get *out* of it. The analysis indicated that had Rudy Price pitched the nose higher and firewalled the throttles, all would have been well. The L1011 would have cleared the plowed field, flown off into the setting sun,

111

and landed at DFW without a scratch. The report was tidy, neat, mathematically meticulous. Disgusted pilots at the NTSB hearing where it was explained saw it as the ultimate triumph of computer logic over real-world experience. Connors and Price were not around to suggest that, just perhaps, planes flew better when constructed of perforated computer forms than aluminum and steel.

NASA engineer James Bray, the man who headed the analysis, testified at the hearing that his calculations, which were based on the information obtained from the DFDR, showed that "the airplane physically had the performance capability to fly a path that missed the ground. In fact, the records show that the airplane hit the ground with a very modest descent rate, came close to missing the ground."

The spectre of "pilot error" was alive and well in the wake of Bray's testimony. On Friday, November 1, 1985, a story in the *Dallas Morning News* began: "The pilots of Delta Airlines Flight 191 apparently did not try to use 'recovery' techniques—which Delta and other airlines teach their pilots to fly through severe wind shears—according to experts who testified Thursday before the National Transportation Safety Board."

Representatives of the Air Line Pilots Association (ALPA) were particularly perturbed by the thrust of the NASA analysis, one that had yet to be tested. Delta Captain Bill Melvin, one of the foremost authorities on wind shear in the United States, said, "You write this accident off as pilot error, and you're just inviting other pilots to try to fly through a microburst."

After the hearing, NASA's wind model was put to the test in three different types of simulators. Boeing plugged the data into its 727 and 747 simulators, while United used its trijet DC-10, which most nearly approximates the performance of the TriStar. Simulators offer pilots a sweaty-palmed realism available in only one other place: the cockpit of an airplane aloft. Once the door is closed in a modern simulator, the sounds, sights, and feel are all "real." Actual airborne training duplications of failed engines and other emergencies are things of the past. Airlines lost too many pilots, too many multimillion-dollar flying machines that way. A "crash" in a simulator might leave a pilot weak-kneed, but at least he could stumble away to the bathroom.

112 NTSB aerospace engineer Gorney was one of the pilots who flew the 191 profile. The results: "It was really quite a ride. Gave you a real headache. I can say that everybody was really shaking their heads. If this, in fact, really duplicates the winds that 191 experienced, nobody could confidently make it through every time. In fact, one test pilot got in and flew it through successfully the first time and crashed it the second. I crashed it the first two times and finally made it through the third. But I wouldn't bet my money that I could make it through the fourth."

In perspective, Gorney and the other pilots knew what they were getting into. Connors and Price didn't.

In a shear, a really bad one, the dynamics of stall speed and attitude go out the window. "Yeah," agrees Gorney. "The thing that was so disconcerting here is that the airplane is bouncing around quite a bit. You're getting stickshaker [warning of stall] at speeds quite a bit higher than normal. . . . Because of the severity of the up- and downdrafts, that changes your angle of attack drastically. Really, there's one common thread about stall. You stall the airplane when you reach what's called the 'critical angle of attack' [the angle of the wings relative to the wind]. If you go beyond that, the airplane stalls. That critical angle varies with certain parameters. Once you introduce a strong downdraft in there, the airplane is going to be at a very low angle of attack. You put updrafts in there, the airplane is going to be at higher angles of attack."

When the stickshaker activated on the simulations, it was at speeds considerably higher than the pilot had any reason to expect. The natural reaction was to ease off the stickshaker (to keep from stalling) by lowering the nose. "But," cautions Gorney, "it's one thing to say it and another thing to do it. Because if you push it [the yoke] forward, the nose of the airplane really wants to drop over on ya'."

The common thread that ran through the few instances in which pilots did successfully challenge the killer of 191 was that "when you got stickshaker, you did not nose over the aircraft." The tricky technique, even in a ground-bound simulator, is more easily reflected upon than accomplished. Says Gorney, "Sometimes, just to hold it [the nose] nowhere near the stickshaker, just to hold it five degrees, I had the damn control column back in my gut."

There is substantial evidence that Connors and Price attempted to fly proper wind shear recovery technique, while at the same time trying to prevent what would certainly have been an absolutely fatal stall, a catastrophe from which no one would have walked away. In all probability, it was vortex rolls—the chaotic lashings of the microburst—that spawned the violent up- and downdrafts and ultimately turned their world upside down. In his book *DFW Microburst*, Dr. Ted Fujita theorizes that there were three vortices.

One key to escaping a severe shear is early recognition. To that end, Piedmont Airlines, the expanding domestic carrier based in Charlotte, North Carolina, has become the first airline in the world to install wind shear detection devices on a regular operational basis on its fleet. The computerized system was tested on Piedmont planes for months before the FAA certificated it on November 5, 1985. The Sperry system costs between $100,000 and $125,000 per plane. The warning consists of lights, a voice, and, eventually, a feature that tells the pilot which angle of attack will get him out.

An amber light first warns of impending shear. If it's a strong one, a red light appears along with a recorded voice that repeats the phrase "wind shear" until, and if, the plane successfully makes it through the thing.

Piedmont is pioneering the device; no FAA regulation says they must. In fact, no regulation mandates wind shear detection systems of *any* kind. In 1982 the FAA issued a Notice of Proposed Rule Making that said it intended to require the installation of airborne wind shear warning technology. In 1984 the agency issued Advisory Bulletin 120-41, which outlined the criteria for the manufacture of wind shear alerting systems. Since then, they have decreed nothing. The idea seems to have fallen between the bureaucratic cracks.

Sperry is not the only company with a product ready to plug into existing aircraft. A pioneer in the field, Safe Flight Instrument Corporation, markets what it calls a Wind Shear Warning/Recovery Guidance System (WSW/RG) for around $14,000 per unit. The computer device provides crews with voice alert when they are on the verge of a shear. Then automatic pitch guidance clicks in, pointing the way to escape.

In 1981 Leonard Greene, the man who heads Safe Flight, received the Flight Safety Foundation's Award for Meritorious Service for the development of the WSW/RG. Still, against all logic, the system languishes. It costs less than some in-flight movie setups, is capable of saving a planeload of people, and—as far as the airline community is concerned—goes virtually unused. In the cost-conscious milieu of post-deregulation commercial aviation, has operational safety taken a back seat to marketing sizzle? The concentration on in-flight passenger amenities and ignorance of potentially lifesaving equipment does little to refute the notion. There may be no regulation that says that airlines must employ detection devices, but—as Piedmont admirably demonstrates—there is no law against it, either.

The Safe Flight system has been certified for use on 727s, 747s, and the Air Force's C-135, used by the joint chiefs of staff. In addition, it is in place and operating on business jets across the world. Ironically, six IBM executives and their wives died on Flight 191. Some contend that had they been flying a company craft, they would have been alive today: IBM's corporate fleet is equipped with wind shear detection devices.

The prime criticism of present airborne wind shear detection systems is that they aren't *predictive*. Once a pilot has started into a shear, they do provide recognition and a bit of warning before the lift-killing tailwind takes hold; but it is almost after the fact: "Here you are. Here's how to get out." To that Greene counters, "The question should be not whether a system is labeled 'predictive' or 'reactive,' but whether it can prevent wind shear crashes."

Safe Flight has already proven, via simulation, that the WSW/RG is a reliable, extraordinarily useful tool. It works. Thus, perhaps the next question is, does it work in all circumstances, in all intensities of shears? Can the pilot be assured of escape if he simply follows the pitch guidance and applies full power? The answer to

114

that is no. Certain microbursts, encountered at certain altitudes, are killers, no matter whether the pilot has warning or follows recommended procedures. Reactive in-flight detection is not a panacea, nor is improved training for crews. They are simply elements in a triad, the key to which is predictive detection of microbursts, followed by absolute avoidance.

After the crash of Eastern Flight 66 in 1975, the FAA began to install Low Level Wind Shear Alert Systems at a number of airports across the country. In all, 110 facilities either have or are slated to get LLWSAS. The system consists of a series of anemometers, or wind gauges, linked to a central computer. When wind differentials greater than 15 knots are recorded, the control tower is alerted.

There are, however, blind spots in the system. First, sensors record only shears at the airport itself, not on critical approach paths. The LLWSAS at DFW, for example, alerted controllers only after 191 had crashed. Second, at larger airports, microbursts can actually pass between sensors, undetected.

In 1982, about the time Pan Am 759 crashed, a definitive counter to the killer was being developed in Colorado, an area especially susceptible to shear. The project was called JAWS, an acronym for Joint Airport Weather Studies. The idea was to develop a Doppler radar system capable of identifying and tracking microbursts. Traditional weather radar is virtually blind to the virulent phenomenon. Doppler radar unmasks it. The technology is named for Johann Christian Doppler, who discovered in 1842 that an object's speed and direction can be determined by the wavelengths it emits, be they sound waves, light waves, or radio waves. Applied to radar, the Doppler principle can tell whether wind-borne moisture is moving in two directions at once—the telltale signature of a microburst.

JAWS detected 160 microbursts in 91 days. Still, the system was purely experimental. It was not until after May 31, 1984—the day a United 727 narrowly escaped a savage shear at Denver's Stapleton International Airport—that the FAA asked for an operational study. John McCarthy of the National Center for Atmospheric Research headed the original JAWS team and its operational reincarnation, CLAWS. The acronym stands for Classify, Locate, and Avoid Wind Shear. CLAWS lasted for forty-five days and was centered at Stapleton. "It was enormously successful," maintains McCarthy. "We issued microburst advisories with an average of two to four minutes advance warning to pilots, whereas LLWSAS was running about one minute late in every case."

115

How does this translate into human terms? "One pilot," says the young scientist, "reported to us—he believes—that [a wind shear] advisory saved his airplane." The aircraft was on approach to Stapleton. Forty-five days of CLAWS cost the FAA $300,000. For that price, the federal government saved the lives of a planeload full of people.

Why did the effort end? "We were expecting to continue it and they [the FAA] said they ran out of money," says McCarthy. Is he frustrated? "Sure. I've been working with this problem for some years. I'm a goal-oriented person. I want to see the job finished." McCarthy believes that Doppler systems could be installed at airports for about $3 million each. The technology is there. "But we still have to finish the job of making it operationally useful in a routine manner."

To a degree, that's where Memphis entered into the picture. The city was the site of yet another Doppler project. One problem with the system is ground clutter, "too much return from trees, buildings, and so on," says McCarthy. This makes microburst detection difficult. The Memphis mission was to determine whether clutter could be sufficiently suppressed. It can. "That radar has been operating all this summer [1985] most successfully."

Yet the Memphis system was sterile. It provided "neither ATC [Air Traffic Control] nor pilot product." The radar dish simply went around and around collecting data. It wasn't hooked up to the tower. After the ground clutter obstacle had been surmounted, the next hurdle lay in fine-tuning the transfer of useful information from the system to the pilot. CLAWS was a labor-intensive effort employing Ph.D.s and meteorologists in the Stapleton tower.

The process is impractical on a widespread basis. McCarthy believes that automation is the key: "The fact that we can transfer it [microburst information] to pilots in a timely manner fundamentally is resolved. Still to be resolved, and fully tractable, is putting the resources into an operational test facility where you attempt to automate this information. That," says McCarthy, "is where the ball game lies."

It also lies with money.

The American flying public has been bilked. Eight percent of the price of every airline ticket purchased goes to something called the Airport and Airways Trust Fund. The program was renewed and taxes substantially raised in 1981 with the idea of modernizing the air traffic control system and increasing airport capacity. The revenues of this ambitious program were earmarked to fund things like computers, runways, and radar— Doppler included.

116 During the 1984–85 fiscal year, more than $3 billion was raised. Sources on Capitol Hill say that Congress authorized $1.3 billion for the FAA. Only $750 million of that was spent. Yet the agency "ran out" of money for the CLAWS program, an effort that had already proven itself to be a lifesaver!

The bureaucratic sleight-of-hand that produced these numbers was prompted by the voracious federal deficit, a colossus that swallows whole not only antipoverty programs, but airplanes. The revenues from the user tax—for accounting purposes— go to the trust fund, but the money itself is thrown into the maw of the congressional appropriations process. When the trust fund's income exceeds outgo, the surplus is credited against the deficit—neat, especially if you have a hand in controlling that surplus.

Enter OMB, the Office of Management and Budget. The president's fiscal watchdog plays a major role in helping determine what will and will not be spent. And Terminal Doppler Radar, the kind designed to detect low-level wind shear, has gotten short shrift.

The *Washington Post* quoted one safety-conscious OMB official as saying, "You can take all the people who were killed in the Delta accident. More people were killed on motorcycles last week. How safe is safe?" An FAA official recounted that OMB told him, "The one problem holding this [Terminal Doppler] up is that you guys don't have enough accidents."

Terminal Doppler was initially wedded to a larger, continent-spanning effort called NEXRAD, short for Next Generation Radar. NEXRAD is a long-range system (145 to 290 miles) of 130 weather surveillance radars. It will help weather forecasters better identify tornadoes, gust fronts, and severe atmospheric turbulence. NEXRAD will provide better overall aviation weather information, primarily for flights en route, but it won't identify localized microbursts that threaten airports.

Terminal Doppler would have a range of twelve miles. Its purpose is limited: to detect microbursts. The technology is nearly the same for the two systems, but there are important differences in wavelength and rate of scan. Terminal Doppler must search much more frequently over a limited area to provide the kind of microburst warning that pilots need.

OMB held up the NEXRAD program, and thus Terminal Doppler, for several months when it ordered the three federal agencies involved—the departments of Commerce, Transportation, and Defense—to review whether cheaper "off-the-shelf," rather than developmental technology, would suffice. Ostensibly, the idea was to save money. However, the three departments had already determined that ready-to-wear would not work.

The bureaucracies complied with the "off-the-shelf" review, coming to the conclusion that virtually everyone knew they would: existing Doppler technology would not do the job. There are those in Congress who believed that the OMB move **117** was simply a bureaucratic fudge, a tactic meant ultimately to wither the project by studying it to death. One of them is Norman Mineta (D-Cal.). The energetic chairman of the House Subcommittee on Aviation and former mayor of San Jose is one of the highest-ranking Japanese-Americans in Congress and a frequent flyer. When he travels home to California's 13th Congressional District, he often sits in a cockpit "jumpseat"—right behind the pilots. After the crash of Delta 191, he "flew" a simulator through wind shear conditions. His interest in and familiarity with commercial aviation goes considerably beyond staff-generated briefing papers. In a statement before his own subcommittee, Mineta said, "The Office of Management and Budget will not be satisfied [with the "off-the-shelf" cost review] and will continue to scale down the NEXRAD program now and the Terminal Doppler Radar Program in the future. My concern is that the OMB will drop the next shoe and tell the agencies that their needs are too rich and exorbitant and that they should scale back their plans. If OMB fails to get reports which show that a scaled-back technology will meet the agencies' needs, I am afraid that OMB will attack the needs themselves. My suspicion is that the review OMB has requested is only Chapter One of the Administration's true intents and purposes."

Mineta went on to challenge what he called the "get-the-government-out-of-everything" philosophy of the early 1980s, saying, "The detection of tornadoes, flood, or wind shear, and the dissemination of information about those hazardous weather phenomena, are functions which cannot be left to the marketplace. If the government steps back from these responsibilities, I am not certain they will be done effectively. If they are not, it will be tremendously costly to the public, industry and the federal government. To not adequately deal with harzardous weather detection would be very short-sighted, and in the end, costly to everyone—in terms of dollars and in terms of lives."

Ironically, the very free-market expansion fostered during the first half of the 1980s would be well served by Terminal Doppler. During the forty-five-day CLAWS project at Stapleton, airlines saved some $875,000 in fuel alone because of the operational use of Terminal Doppler. Assigned takeoff and landing runways, if seen to be affected by wind shear, were changed in advance. Not only did this save airplanes, but it also avoided delays and fuel burned through holds and diversions. Despite the recent drop in Jet A fuel prices, fuel still accounts for a huge percentage of an airline's operating expenses.

The FAA estimates that it will cost some $500 million to install Terminal Doppler at 110 of the nation's major airports. Based on the savings generated by the six-week operational study at Stapleton alone, Dr. John McCarthy contends, "It doesn't take very long for a system to pay for itself in simple efficiency improvements." So much for "cost-effectiveness."

118

At the end of fiscal year 1985, there was a $3.3 billion surplus in the Airport and Airway Trust Fund. Congressman Mineta estimates that by the end of fiscal year 1986 it will have ballooned to $4.6 billion! In a statement before the House Committee on Public Works and Transportation, Mineta said: "With the Trust Fund included in the general Presidential and Congressional budgets, the increase in the Trust Fund's uncommitted surplus has served to reduce the general budget deficit. In other words, since fiscal 1982 aviation users had contributed $1.3 billion to reduce the general budget deficit." His proposal is to remove the fund from the presidential and

Congressional budget process and free the monies to be used for the purposes they were intended: saving lives and improving a severely overtaxed Air Traffic Control system.

As of this writing, funding for Terminal Doppler is still in flux. Feeling the heat of public and congressional pressure, the Reagan administration proposes in its 1987 budget that $55 million be spent for the installation of Terminal Doppler Radar at fifteen airports nationwide, including DFW. The proposal is a token, a far cry from the actual number of units needed. When, where, and perhaps even *if* it will be operationally deployed are questions still very much up in the air. The numbers and timetable are subject to volatile winds, political winds. Only one figure can be counted upon with any degree of certainty: the number of airplanes that will die from microbursts. John McCarthy states firmly: "The statistics state loud and clear that every two or two and a half years we'll have another one."

CONTROLLERS

"This subcommittee has clearly identified the existence of serious and continuing problems of stress, staffing shortages, increasing traffic, lack of supervision and an unseasoned work force. All these factors have combined to produce a diminishing margin of safety in the nation's airways."
—from *Rebuilding the Nation's Air Traffic Control System (Has Safety Taken a Back Seat to Expediency?)*

Some consider the report of the House Subcommittee on Investigations and Oversight a work of immediate, ironic prophecy. It was issued in August 1985. Indications are that an overtaxed air traffic control system may have played a critical role in the death of Delta 191.

The primary job of controllers is to separate airplanes. Everything else is subordinate, including providing pilots with weather information. The more aircraft they handle, the less information they can supply about the weather.

The record of August 2 speaks for itself. As 191 continued on its fatal final approach to Runway 17L, the people in the DFW tower were busy—by some estimates, very busy. Squall lines in East Texas had departing traffic backed up that evening. Because of the logjam, two aircraft nearing touchdown on the airport's east side had to abort their landings. Departing planes blocked the runway. In ATC (air traffic control) jargon, the aborts are called "go-arounds." Minutes after the go-arounds, TRACON (Traffic Control) area supervisor Joe Connors saw something strange on his midfield wind indicator: calm winds with gusts to 14 knots. We pick up his conversation with TRACON/Tower Supervisor Roger Kennedy. The time is 18:01:49; Delta 191 still has more than four minutes of life left. In the cockpit of the craft, *Ted* Connors is lowering the landing gear:

18:01:49—JOE CONNORS: "That wind, is that the reason for the go-around, or what?

121

I see it's calm with gust to fourteen or something. Is that really true, or what?"

18:03:59 – KENNEDY: "You mean the two we had earlier?"

18:02:01 – JOE CONNORS: "Yeah."

18:02:02 – KENNEDY: "I think it was just a hell of a mess up over here on all this stuff on Local East [the last ATC position link for aircraft arriving on DFW's east runways]. I'll let Gene [Skipworth – the Local East controller] talk to you about it later. He was working it."

18:02:08 – JOE CONNORS: "I don't care about that. I just wondered if the wind –"

As a rule, to maximize lift, aircraft land and take off into the wind. A sudden gust could precede a shift in wind direction, perhaps even presage a storm. These, in turn, might mandate new runway assignments for traffic.

18:02:09 – KENNEDY: "No, no, no, no. It wasn't the wind."

18:02:12 – JOE CONNORS: "Wind isn't giving us a problem?"

18:02:13 – KENNEDY: "No. It wasn't the wind that caused the go-around. I'll put it that away."

18:02:16 – JOE CONNORS: "Okay. We'll keep an eye on that. We're getting calm, gust to twelve or ten or something. Must be bullshit."

18:02:21 – KENNEDY: "Okay."

18:02:22 – JOE CONNORS: "Okay. 'Bye."

During the late afternoon, ATC had been busy routing SWAPS, Severe Weather Avoidance Profiles. The squall line in East Texas temporarily closed two of the area's three departure paths. That meant increased separation between outbound aircraft and increased delays. Managing SWAPS can place an extra burden on the ATC system, especially during periods of pronounced traffic.

122

18:03:57 – JOE CONNORS: "TRACON."

18:03:58 – KENNEDY: "We've been busy with these SWAPS and hadn't paid any attention, but that is heavy, heavy rain off the approach end of both runways. Just for your information. Thank you now."

18:04:58 – JOE CONNORS: (Several floors below in the TRACON room, he looks at a radar scope. Illuminated by the revolving wand of light on the screen is a solid mass sitting two miles off the end of 17L.) "Yeah. I can see that now."

As Kennedy tells his ATC colleague about the deluge, the captain of Flight 191 is on the radio with Gene Skipworth, the person controlling the final segment of approach to 17L. Ted Connors has no idea of how heavy the weather really is. A summer shower masks the storm on the other side. Three aircraft immediately ahead of him have gone through the area without a whimper. In a relaxed voice, Connors says: "Tower. Delta One Ninety One Heavy. [Here, "heavy" denotes a widebody aircraft. It has nothing to do with the intensity of precipitation.] Out here in the rain. Feels good."

At 18:04:01 Skipworth tells Connors he is cleared to land. There is no mention of the wall of water that he is about to enter.

Gene Skipworth, a seventeen-year FAA employee, was a supervisor in the tower August 2. Beginning at 14:58, he worked with a developmental controller (a controller undergoing training) on the Local East position. The idea was to provide on-the-job training. Local East controls the runways on the eastern, or Dallas, side of DFW. By 18:00, the volume of traffic had increased markedly. Skipworth relieved the developmental controller and took over Local East himself. When 191 was handed off to him by the controller manning the Arrival One scope, Skipworth concentrated on separating the TriStar from the Learjet that immediately preceded him. The weather was secondary.

The FAA Handbook mandates a minimum separation of three miles between approaching aircraft under the conditions that were in existence at the time. Just before Skipworth took control of 191, Arrival One told Ted Connors to reduce speed to 150 knots. He was gaining on the Lear. A second before being handed off to Skipworth, 191 was slightly more than 2.75 miles behind the business jet. The margin of separation was evaporating. By 18:04:47 the two planes had closed within 2.5 miles of one another. The crew of Delta 963, one of the aircraft that immediately preceded 191, perceived the change, too. Just after landing, 963's copilot told his captain, "They changed separation to two-and-a-half from three miles." "Yeah," replied the captain. "Maybe they ain't doing it right now," responded the copilot, "but I suspect they are; and that's going to make a lot of difference."

At the NTSB hearing following the crash, Skipworth termed the volume of traffic he was handling that evening "moderate." Delta 191 was on the Local East frequency for exactly two minutes before it cartwheeled into the water towers. In those 120 seconds, Skipworth issued instructions to ten different aircraft at intervals ranging from 3 to 21 seconds. The average interval was one instruction every 9.83 seconds. At a place like DFW, that's not extraordinary. Still, there is no doubt that Gene Skipworth was a busy man, especially considering that the gap between some

123

arrivals was down to two and a half miles, half a mile below the margin prescribed by FAA regulations.

Testifying at the hearing, a chain-smoking Skipworth said he saw lightning shoot from a dark cloud north of the airport and observed what "appeared to be a definite wall of rain." The heavy precipitation was also visible on a special radar display in the tower called a BRITE scope. Although designed primarily to depict air traffic, it can "paint" heavier levels of rain. Still, the controller issued no warnings. Under one interpretation of the FAA regulations, he may not have had to.

Paragraph 2-2b of FAA Handbook 711.65D says: "The primary purpose of the ATC system is to prevent a collision between aircraft operating in the system and to organize and expedite flow of traffic. In addition to its primary function, the ATC system has the capability to provide (with certain limitations) additional services. *The ability to provide additional services is limited by many factors, such as the volume of traffic, frequency congestion, quality of radar, controller workload,* higher priority duties, and the pure physical inability to scan and detect those situations that fall into this category (author's emphasis). It is recognized that these services cannot be provided in cases in which the provision of services is precluded by the above factors. Consistent with the aforementioned conditions, controllers shall provide additional service procedures to the extent permitted by higher priority duties and other circumstances. The provision of additional services is not optional on the part of the controller, but rather is required when the work situation permits."

Weather dissemination, read in this context, can fall into the category of "additional services." Thus, the regulation's translation from bureaucratese reads: "Tell the pilot about weather when you can; but first keep the airplanes from running into one another." The handbook allows controllers considerable leeway: "Each set of circumstances must be evaluated on its own merit and when more than one action is required, the controller shall exercise his best judgment based on the facts and circumstances known to him. That action which is most critical from a safety standpoint is performed first." The question then becomes, was Skipworth, who had seen two go-arounds on Local East a few minutes before, so concerned with keeping 191 from running up the back of the approaching Lear that everything else was secondary? As 191 was in the death-grip of the microburst, the controller—who was unaware as yet of the TriStar's plight—was quickly ordering the Lear off the runway.

"Traffic's a mile final," he radioed the pilot of the corporate jet. Not only was he concerned about separating inbound traffic on 17 Left, but sixteen aircraft were also lined up on taxiways awaiting clearance to depart the companion runway, 17 Right, also under the control of Local East. The Severe Weather Avoidance Profiles initiated earlier in the day because of bad weather in East Texas had DFW traffic backed up on what, under the best of circumstances, would have been one of the busiest periods of the week. The imperative for the veteran controller, indeed the whole DFW ATC setup that evening, was to separate and move traffic.

The letter of the FAA Handbook's ambiguously worded regulation runs counter to the spirit of its Special Bulletin 85-3SP. The bulletin says, in part, "The purpose of this special AT bulletin is to remind all Air Traffic Control Specialists of the upcoming thunderstorm season and the hazardous weather associated with it. Although modern navigational systems and flight techniques make flight into instrument meteorological conditions routine, pilots still must have access to timely and accurate information on the development of thunderstorms in their flight area. The more we understand of the severe atmospheric hazards associated with thunderstorms, the better position we are in to aid the pilot in avoiding these hazards. Because of the severe hazards associated with thunderstorms, *the single most important thing we in the air traffic system can do is help pilots avoid them* (author's emphasis).

During intense questioning at the NTSB hearing, Skipworth never called what he saw outside the tower window a thunderstorm. Although on one occasion he saw lightning, he said that the bolt did not come from the wall of rain. What was the phenomenon observed by the person manning Local East? He said it was a "weather area."

Had Skipworth seen a thunderstorm or related phenomenon, yet another paragraph in the FAA Handbook would have required him to solicit what is called a PIREP—a Pilot Report about weather they have observed. The controller working Local East had neither asked for nor received PIREPs from the aircraft he was handling. Despite FAA insistence that "moderate" traffic prevailed that hot August evening, these facts concerning Local East's workload remain:

1) Separation between 191 and the Lear had been reduced to two and a half miles; 2) two aircraft had to abort their landings and go around minutes before the accident because departing planes blocked the runway; 3) SWAPS had traffic backed up for a significant portion of the afternoon; 4) at the time of the accident, sixteen aircraft—many of them late already—were nose-to-tail awaiting takeoff clearance from Runway 17R; 5) at the time of the crash, ten aircraft were on the Local East radio frequency, not a crush of communication, but not a lax period, either; 6) supervisor Skipworth was handling Local East himself because, as the NTSB's Air Traffic Control Factual Report reads: "The developmental controller had been relieved from the position as the complexity exceeded his capabilities."

ATC may not have told aircraft about the "weather area" off the end of 17L, but it did take direct action to protect the ATC *system* against certain of the afternoon's atmospheric phenomena. Shortly before the crash, a controller who had been on

125

break returned to the TRACON and told area supervisor Joe Connors that he had observed lightning. The controller suggested that the DFW air traffic control facility should fire up its emergency generator. The idea was to be ready in case of a power outage. Connors dialed the number of the facility's environmental specialist. There was no answer. He then paged the man and instructed him to turn on the backup power source.

At the NTSB hearing, Connors testified that he never asked where the lightning was coming from, never associated it with the report of "heavy, heavy rain" from the tower or the solid mass looming off the end of 17L. And yet he put the emergency generator on line.

As with Skipworth's testimony, Joe Connors never referred to the solid echo of "heavy, heavy rain"—the one he saw on the scope shortly after he received word of lightning—as a thunderstorm. It was a "weather area."

The death of Delta 191 bears some startling similarities to, and some significant differences from, a crash that occurred ten years before. John F. Kennedy International Airport, New York, June 24, 1975, 16:05 in the afternoon: Eastern Airlines Flight 66, a Boeing 727 bound from New Orleans, was on final approach to Runway 22L. The trijet penetrated a microburst and dropped below the glideslope. The plane's left wing hit a set of approach lights. Then the 727 rolled into a steep left bank, gouging an open grave in the earth 340 feet long. Before the tail came to a rest on Rockaway Boulevard, spike-like approach towers and surrounding boulders had shredded the aluminum fuselage and most of its human contents. Initially, 14 people—all seated in the tail section—survived. After burns and trauma took their final toll, the living numbered 9. One hundred thirteen of the 124 on board died.

In its official finding of probable cause, the NTSB said, "Contributing to the accident was the continued use of runway 22L when it should have become evident to both air traffic control and the flightcrew that a severe weather hazard existed along the approach path."

Some eight minutes before the accident, National Weather Service radar showed a line of thunderstorms centered along the northern edge of JFK. The stuff was moving southeast and merged just over the approach to 22L. The information was not made available to air traffic control. What had been made available to ATC was a strong wind warning. However, the Kennedy tower failed to pass it along to flight crews operating in the area.

JFK was a busy place that afternoon. The assistant tower chief told the NTSB that shortly after 15:00, he saw thunderstorms to the northwest on radar. After that, he was preoccupied coordinating tower activities and didn't notice rain and lightning north of the airport. The Local control coordinator also saw the storm, replete with lightning, moving in from the north. In the ten to fifteen minutes before the accident,

126

he described the rain as forming a solid wall looming just off the approach end of 22L. He also said he and the Local controller had their hands full controlling traffic.

The Local controller, the man in charge of the final approach leg to 22L, saw the storm. But, like the coordinator, he was busy—too busy to pass on a couple of PIREPS to the tower chief. The PIREPS came from two craft that preceded Eastern 66 on final approach. They spoke of wind shear.

At 15:57:30, just after landing, Flying Tiger Line Flight 161, a DC-8, told the Local controller (LC):

"I just highly recommend that you change the runways and . . . land north-west, you have a tremendous wind shear down near . . . the ground on final."

LC: "Okay, we're indicating wind right down the runway at 15 knots when you landed."

161: "I don't care what you're indicating; I'm just telling you that there's such a wind shear on final that you should change it to the northwest."

LC: (No response.)

At l5:57:30 the Local controller transmitted missed approach instructions to Eastern 902, an L1011 TriStar:

LC: ". . . was wind a problem?"

902: "Affirmative."

"Affirmative." The word spoke volumes. On approach to 22L, the TriStar hit heavy rain at 400 feet. Indicated Air Speed dropped from 150 to 120 knots in seconds, and the widebody began to fall from the sky. A bare 75 feet from disaster, the crew—after applying near maximum thrust and pitching the craft's nose toward the sky—was able to arrest the death drop.

Two other planes, a Finnair DC-8 and a private Beech Baron, followed Eastern 902. They elected to penetrate the shear, adding substantial speed to cope with the anticipated airspeed loss. Both had heard the exchange between 902 and air traffic control. So had Eastern 66.

While there are stark similarities between some aspects of the weather and ATC situations at JFK and DFW, the cockpit voice recordings of the final minutes of Eastern 66 and Delta 191 are studies in contrast. John Kleven, the pilot of the Eastern craft, knew that wind shear lay in wait. Captain Ted Connors didn't:

16:00:27—(EA 902 report of wind shear condition on Kennedy radar frequency.)

16:00:33 – PILOT KLEVEN TO HIS COCKPIT CREW: "You know, this is asinine."

Response from unidentified crewmember: "I wonder if they're covering for themselves?"

16:01:17.5 – COPILOT WILLIAM EBERHART: (he was actually flying the plane): "I'll just fly the glideslope on down, fifteen [degrees of flap deployment], please."

KLEVEN: "Fifteen."

16:01:49.5 – EBERHART: "Final [landing] check when ready."

16:01:54.5 – (sound of altitude monitor).

KLEVEN: "It's on."

FLIGHT ENGINEER: "Speedbrake."

KLEVEN: "Forward detent."

FLIGHT ENGINEER: "Radar."

KLEVEN: "Up and off. Ah, standby."

16:02:12.5 – FLIGHT ENGINEER: "Gear down."

16:02:20.0 – KLEVEN: "Five Rel. I have the radar on standby in case I need it. I can get it off later." (This could suggest that Kleven was thinking about the possibility of not making the approach or having to abandon it.)

16:02:27.5 – KLEVEN: "They're [the flaps], uh, fifteen [degrees]. And standby."

16:02:36.0 – FLIGHT ENGINEER: "That valve light came back on, John."

16:02:42.0 – JFK ATC TO EASTERN 902: "Roger Eastern nine zero two. Would you classify that as a severe wind shift, uh correction – shear?"

16:02:47.5 – 902 TO JFK: "Affirmative."

128 16:02:50.5 – COPILOT EBERHART: "Gonna keep a pretty healthy margin [of speed] on this one."

Response from unidentified crewmember: "I, uh, would suggest that you do."

EBERHART: "In case he's right."

He is. Just how right begins to become apparent two minutes later:

16:04:52.6 – KLEVEN (WHO IS SQUINTING OUT AT A RAIN-STREAKED WINDSCREEN) TELLS

COPILOT EBERHART: "I have approach lights [in sight]."

16:04:53.2 – EBERHART: "Okay."

16:04:54.7 – KLEVEN: "Stay on the gauges." (Eberhart is monitoring the instruments while Kleven monitors the landing visually through the windscreen. The copilot had his "head in the cockpit.")

16:04:55.8 – EBERHART: "I'm with it."

As Eberhart acknowledges Kleven's instructions, his airspeed plummets by 20 knots. The very fabric of the air itself is ripped, and Flight 66 is falling through the crack:

16:05:06.2 – KLEVEN: "Runway in sight."

16:05:07.1 – EBERHART: "I got it."

16:05:09.3 – KLEVEN: "Got it?"

16:05:10.2 – EBERHART: "Takeoff thrust!"

The copilot realizes their plight. His command is moot. From somewhere in the cockpit a crewmember cries out. The CVR records the onset of Flight 66's death throes at precisely 16:05:11.4

The final decision to land on 22L, to penetrate the known shear, was the pilot-in-command's. ATC didn't force Eastern 66 to continue on final approach. Still, the system played a part. While ATC cannot prevent a pilot from landing, it can change runway assignments.

The afternoon of June 24, 1975, was a busy one at JFK. Changing the assignments and landing planes in the opposite direction, as suggested by the Flying Tiger pilot, would no doubt have caused some delays, inconvenienced connecting passengers, and added to an already bloated controller workload. The alternative was business as usual, thunderstorm or not.

Commenting in the wake of Eastern 66, some ten years before 191, the **129** NTSB said: "ATC must recognize that thunderstorms and other dynamic weather conditions which develop within, or move into, terminal areas may seriously disrupt the safe flow of traffic. When these conditions appear likely, ATC must be capable of adjusting the flow of traffic in terminal areas so that timely actions and rational judgments in the interest of air safety are primary to moving the traffic."

It is important to note that, as of this writing, neither official nor legal blame has been attached to either the FAA's role or that of individual controllers concerning the events of August 2. At least one investigator close to the case says that the controllers at DFW are "clean" as far as any responsibility is concerned. Whatever actions controllers did or did not take that fateful afternoon, they—like their counterparts at JFK ten years earlier—fulfilled their primary mandate: they separated traffic. Not everybody in the ATC system can make that statement.

"It was within 50 to 100 feet of becoming the worst aviation accident in U.S. history." So spoke NTSB chairman Jim Burnett in the wake of the near-collision of two widebody DC-10s March 31, 1985, at Minneapolis–St. Paul International Airport (MSP).

It is nighttime at the sprawling Twin Cities hub, home of Northwest Orient Airlines. Two of its DC-10s, Flights 51 and 65, are preparing for takeoff. Between them, the two "heavy" jets are carrying 502 passengers. Inside the two cockpits, everything is routine.

21:03:37 – MSP TOWER TO NORTHWEST 51: "Northwest fifty-one heavy, runway to nine left. There's traffic crossing down field. Fly the runway heading and cleared for takeoff."

21:03:38 – MSP GROUND CONTROL TO NORTHWEST 65: "Northwest, ah, sixty-five heavy, taxi across two nine left."

21:03:39 – CAPTAIN OF NORTHWEST 65 TO HIS COPILOT: "He didn't clear us to cross, did he?"

21:03:40 – COPILOT'S RESPONSE: "No."

21:03:42 – AGAIN, MSP GROUND CONTROL TO NORTHWEST 65: "Northwest sixty-five heavy, cross two nine left."

21:03:43 – COPILOT OF NORTHWEST 65 TO MINNEAPOLIS GROUND CONTROL: "To cross two nine. Northwest sixty-five heavy."

At the same instant, Northwest 51 is acknowledging the apparent takeoff clearance from MSP Tower.

130

21:03:43 – FLIGHT 51'S COPILOT TO MSP TOWER: "Runway heading. Cleared for takeoff, Northwest fifty-one heavy."

Inside Flight 51's cockpit, the flight engineer goes through last-second checks.

21:03:46 – NORTHWEST 51'S ENGINEER TO THE REST OF THE COCKPIT CREW: "Bleed's off—High intensity lights are on—Takeoff checks complete."

At 21:03:50, the sound of engine power increase is heard on the CVR as Flight 51 begins its takeoff roll.

21:03:49 – An unidentified cockpit crewmember of Northwest 65: "See this guy comin' down the runway."

21:03:59 – Northwest 51 continues to roll. A voice in the cockpit calls out: "One fourty-five – looks good."

21:04:03 – The copilot of Flight 51 calls out the speed of the barreling behemoth: "There's one hundred knots."

21:04:00 – An unidentified voice from the flight deck of Northwest 65: "He's turning off."

21:04:06 – The copilot of Flight 51 sees Northwest 65: "Is he gonna stop – or not?"

21:04:09 – Northwest 51's flight engineer tells Captain Donald Nelson: "Don, there's a whale goin' right across the runway."

21:04:09 – At the same instant, Nelson says: "Yeah."

21:04:12 – NELSON: "I see him."

21:04:13 – NELSON: "Yeah. We're gonna do it [take off] here."

21:04:15 – FLIGHT 51'S COPILOT: "Jesus Christ."

21:04:16 – NELSON ORDERS: "Rotate." Flight 51 lumbers into the cold northern night.

21:04:20 – NELSON: "Okay."

21:04:20 – As Flight 51 pulls up, the engineer of Northwest 65 realizes what's happening: "Who, ah – Who, ah. Who?"

21:04:21 – FLIGHT ENGINEER OF NORTHWEST 51: "How about a gear."

21:04:22 – CAPTAIN NELSON COMPLIES: "Gear up."

131

21:04:22 – By now, the copilot of Flight 65 also sees the barely airborne apparition: "Oh! Oh!"

21:04:23 – NORTHWEST 65'S CAPTAIN: "Jesus Christ."

21:04:24 to 21:04:27 – The DC-10's three power levers (throttles) are rammed forward as the takeoff warning horn blares in the cockpit. The engines shriek. The crew of Flight 65 is desperately trying to get out of the way.

21:04:28 – NORTHWEST 51 CAPTAIN DON NELSON: "There's no way we could have stopped."

21:04:30 – HIS FLIGHT ENGINEER: "No."

21:04:31 – FLIGHT 51'S COPILOT TO MSP TOWER: "Was, ah, the [DC] ten cleared to cross?"

21:04:35 – TOWER: "Northwest fifty-one. Yes sir. He was cleared to cross."

21:04:39 – TOWER: "Northwest Fifty-one heavy, you fly the runway heading and contact departure."

21:04:42 – Flight 51's copilot acknowledges the instructions: "Fifty-one heavy."

21:04:28 – The captain of Flight 65 exclaims: "Holy ## [non-pertinent word]!"

21:04:28 – At the same moment, his copilot radioes: "Tower, you know what you just did?" There is no response.

21:04:34 – The copilot calls MSP ground control: "Ground, Northwest sixty-five heavy."

21:04:36 – MSP GROUND CONTROL: "Northwest sixty-five heavy. Ah, roger. Stand by."

21:04:42 – 51'S COPILOT: "Holy –."

21:04:43 – 51'S CAPTAIN: "Jesus Christ."

21:04:45 – An altogether different sound fills the cockpit: laughter.

Why didn't Captain Nelson simply elect to abort the takeoff? He says the Twin Cities airport was simply too crowded: "My peripheral vision said there was a lot of traffic to the left and to the right," said Nelson in testimony before James Oberstar's (D-Minn.) House Subcommittee on Oversight and Investigations. Aborting the takeoff might have taken the DC-10 off the runway and into other airplanes. At the point Flight 51 cleared the other Northwest jet, seven other aircraft were within 500 feet. They could have become involved in secondary impacts or fires. The crew's decisive judgment and consummate skill averted what could have been the worst crash in the history of aviation. The margin of life for perhaps more than a thousand human beings was somewhere around fifty feet.

Minneapolis–St. Paul is usually a busy place. The night of March 31, things were more harried than usual. NTSB chairman Burnett told Oberstar's subcommittee that a snowstorm had hit the area. Airlines had asked permission of the FAA to land as many flights as possible at MSP because of the stormy weather. The FAA said yes.

"The consequence," said the NTSB chief, "was to increase the number of planes on the ground perhaps beyond the capacity of the airport."

A little over a month later, the same sort of thing happened at Philadelphia. On May 8 a Lufthansa DC-10 had to abort its takeoff when the pilot noticed a Republic DC-9 on the runway. According to investigators, the Lufthansa flight had been cleared for takeoff at the same time the Republic plane was told to cross the runway.

Near-misses on the ground developed into a major safety hazard during 1985. During the first eight months of the year, the incidence was up 37 percent compared with a similar period in 1984. Through August 1985, there were 81 recorded cases in which planes on runways and taxiways came dangerously close to other aircraft or ground vehicles. The NTSB's Burnett thinks 1985 was something more than a statistical aberration: "Clearly we have a trend that the safety board is concerned about. I believe it is a trend. That is very certain." Investigators discovered no geographic pattern to the near-tragedies. They "appear to be randomly spread across the country," testified NTSB official David Kelly. He suggested that some of the occurrences implied "a distinct breakdown between the ground controller and the local controller."

Not all of the ground glitches took place at large, busy airports. Nor were they all bloodless. On June 20, 1985, at Birmingham Municipal Airport, an Alabama National Guard F-4 Phantom plowed into an Airborne Express Beech 18. The F-4 had been cleared to land on Runway 05 after practicing instrument approaches. At the same time, the Beech 18 was cleared for takeoff from an intersection of the same runway. The pilot of the propeller-driven craft died. The crew of the F-4 escaped with minor injuries.

In response to the dramatic upsurge, FAA administrator Donald Engen made conference calls to controllers at more than four hundred towers across the country. He asked for increased vigilance and coordination between ground controllers and those issuing takeoff clearance. During peak periods, he said, a third person should link tower and ground controllers, providing in essence an extra set of eyes.

Statistics concerning near-misses on the ground are sobering. Numbers involving the airborne variety are startling. Early in 1985, the FAA said that there were 292 near-midair collisions in 1984. Later, after probing by Ralph Nader's Aviation Consumer Action Project (ACAP), the agency said that they had been off a bit: by 300, to be precise. The real figure was 592, higher than ever before. In response to the consumer group's criticism, FAA chief Engen decided to order a recount of 1983's near-miss figures. They skyrocketed from 286 to 478.

At the time of the revelation by ACAP, the FAA defined a near-midair collision as occurring anytime a pilot felt his craft was in danger of being hit by another.

Most of the time this means anytime two planes fly within 500 feet of one another. It is important to note that the majority of near-midairs involve private, general aviation aircraft, flying under Visual Flight Rules (VFR). Under such circumstances, the rule is see and be seen. However, incidents involving commercial airliners under positive ground control have been frighteningly evident in recent years.

On June 20, 1985, the same day that the National Guard F-4 rammed the Beech in Birmingham, two Eastern jets came within 300 feet of colliding with one another. The place was the crowded Northeast Corridor, a network of routes stretching from Washington, D.C., to Boston. An Eastern 727 shuttle bound from Washington National Airport to New York La Guardia was at Flight Level 70 (7,000 feet) when the pilot saw one of his company's A300 Airbuses climbing toward him. The shuttle pilot wrenched the trijet 727 into an evasive climb, averting disaster. As of this writing, no blame has been assessed in the incident.

On the same day as the Eastern incident, an American Airlines 727 descending over Lake Michigan had to take evasive action to avoid a twin-engine private plane. During the hearings that preceded the writing of *Rebuilding the Nation's Air Traffic Control System*, the subcommittee played a tape that frighteningly illustrates the post–PATCO strike gremlin of inexperience. The incident happened in Los Angeles. A DC-10 was cleared for takeoff by a developmental controller. A KC-10 military craft was making a low-level, high-speed approach to the airport at about the same time and in the same direction. The relatively inexperienced developmental controller was alerted to the potential problem by a controller manning a radar in the TRACON. "Aw, shit, it's not working out at all," excitedly responded the controller in the tower. Then he told the TRACON controller, "You gotta do something now." The subcommittee report states, "An alternate course of action was worked out and a potential mishap was avoided."

The FAA never investigated the incident. Subsequently, the same tower controller was promoted. A year after the incident, while giving on-the-job training to a developmental controller, he told two aircraft to use the same taxiway at the same time. The two jets ran into one another. One lost three feet of wing, while the other suffered severe damage to leading-edge lift devices on one of its wings.

On August 3, 1981, four years and a day before the crash of Delta 191, the Professional Air Traffic Controllers Organization (PATCO) went on strike. At that time, the FAA employed some 16,375 controllers. According to agency statistics, 13,311 of those were "full performance" (i.e., fully certified to operate all positions in a defined area). In August 1985, the FAA had 14,043 controllers, but only 8,374 of them were experienced, full-performance-rated controllers. That's a 37 percent *decrease* as compared to 1981.

The year of the PATCO walkout, United States scheduled airlines flew some

249 billion revenue passenger miles. A revenue passenger mile, or rpm, is defined as one paying passenger transported one mile. It's a basic measure of industry health. In terms of rpm's, 1985 was a record year for U.S. airlines. The Air Transport Association estimates that more than 330 billion rpm's were logged, a 33 percent *increase* over 1981 figures. In other words, while more passengers flew in more airplanes than ever before during the first half of the decade, the number of fully qualified people handling those planes—protecting the passengers—plummeted.

In response to the sobering figures, transportation secretary Elizabeth Dole responded with numbers of her own. She said the FAA would phase in 1,000 controllers during fiscal years 1986 and 1987. That would mean, ostensibly, that by September 30, 1988 (the end of the 1987 fiscal year), there would be more than 15,000 controllers working traffic, still fewer than the number employed before the PATCO strike. Even the 15,000 count, however, does not take into account attrition sparked by stress, retirement, and other factors. A survey by the General Accounting Office, the government's watchdog agency, casts a shadow on FAA projections. For the survey, GAO sent questionnaires to some 4,500 full-performance and developmental controllers, in addition to 1,000 first-line supervisors. Of the 5,500 questionnaires sent out, GAO received some 4,200 responses. Testifying before Senator Nancy Kassebaum's (R-Kan.) Senate Aviation Subcommittee, a GAO official said: "The rebuilding process is also complicated by the fact that FAA may lose many of its experienced controllers and supervisors through retirement. About 15 percent [of those surveyed] or 570 controllers responded that they will be eligible to retire within two years, and of that number 84 percent said they would probably retire. Percentagewise, attrition of first-line supervisors could be much greater. Of 880 supervisors responding, half said they will reach retirement eligibility within two years; of that number, 81 percent said they probably will retire. *Supervisors reported that they spend about 36 percent of their time actually controlling traffic*" [author's emphasis].

It seems clear that, barring a significant downturn in the economy, the volume of air traffic can be expected to continue to rise during the last half of the decade. Indications are that there simply will not be enough people around to handle it all.

The FAA is pinning its future ability to handle air traffic on a $9 billion wonderwork called the National Airspace System, or NAS Plan. The idea is to automate the ATC system with computers and advanced solid-state technology. The existing system of Air Route Traffic Control Centers (ARTCCs), which guide aircraft between cities and airport-based TRACONs, would be consolidated into a much smaller network of regional or dual-function facilities. The FAA estimates that once the NAS Plan is fully implemented by the year 2000, it will have saved taxpayers $22 billion. By then, perhaps controller overwork and stress will be things of the past. Perhaps. But for the

135

next few years, these factors—coupled with retirements—will continue to put pressure on the ATC system. The NAS Plan's first real labor-saving features will not begin to make a significant impact until the early 1990s.

In the mid-1970s the FAA commissioned a study of controller stress that came to be known as the Rose Report. Among the findings were that controllers had excessive incidences of high blood pressure, a precursor to cardiovascular problems. Also, they had higher-than-average incidences of psychological and personal problems. These included alcohol abuse, chronic depression, and impulsivity. Testifying before Congress, Dr. Rose said, "Controllers are very negativistic about themselves as well as about the agency [the FAA]. That's one of their major problems." Rose said that during his study, controllers repeatedly told him, "Doc, it's not the job. It's the system."

Among Rose's recommendations to help ease stress were "biofeedback and meditation/relaxation" to control high blood pressure and "standard professional help routinely offered," as well as a "widespread network of counseling services" to ease psychological problems.

After spending $2.8 million on the study, the FAA ignored its findings. An excerpt from *Rebuilding the Nation's Air Traffic Control System:* "Dr. Stanley Mohler, FAA's technical officer for the Rose Study, had the responsibility of monitoring the study to assure that it was well-conducted and met FAA's needs. Dr. Mohler's testimony shed some light on why FAA did not utilize the study. Mohler, who had left the FAA prior to his testimony, stated that each office in FAA accepted the original Rose Report except the sections affecting them, with which they were unhappy. For example, the medical office 'didn't like the concepts relating to stress,' and some in the office 'denied that there was such a phenomenon as stress.' In fact, the medical scientists at the Civil Aeromedical Institute in Oklahoma City 'were ordered to delete the word from their manuscripts for a period, which I thought was kind of interesting.'"

Testifying before the Oversight and Investigations Subcommittee in May 1983, transportation secretary Dole defended the FAA when she testified, "No one has found a way to quantify stress." She went on to say, "There has just not been evidence produced that there really is unique stress [involved with being a controller]." The official line was, ignore it and it will go away.

Within a year, high-ranking officials seemed to have changed their minds. The acting administrator of the FAA told the committee that the agency was moving ahead with an "imaginative and effective program" to alleviate stress. Despite the welcome pronouncement, the subcommittee remained less than totally convinced that "specific FAA activities" were "seriously" addressing the problem.

Rebuilding the Nation's Air Traffic Control System highlights the shortage of experienced controllers, the heavy workloads, continued stress, and soaring reports of near-midair collisions. But how do controllers themselves feel about things? Privately, more than one told this author, "We're in a hell of a mess." More formally, they sounded off via the questionnaire developed by the GAO. Some key findings included the following:

1) "70 percent of the radar controllers believe they are required to handle more traffic during daily peak periods than they should be handling. Their supervisors said that a much lower percentage – 38 percent of the controllers under their supervision – are required to handle too much traffic, but even their estimate represents over 2,000 controllers." 2) "69 percent of controllers believe that the heavy workload is adversely affecting the safety of the system." 3) "In rating the quality of training for controlling traffic *in bad weather* [author's emphasis], 35 percent of the supervisors and 55 percent of the controllers rated it less than adequate to poor."

There are deep-rooted, sometimes fatal flaws in the fabric of our air traffic control system. The question is, how do we mend them? The Investigations and Oversight Subcommittee had a number of recommendations. Perhaps the most important concern capacity, human and systemic:

Stress:

"1) Accept stress as a major problem affecting controllers. 2) Reduce stress by developing a well-thought-out program that: a) Addresses stress-causing conditions in the control environment, particularly poor human relations management and too much traffic; b) Mitigates the psychological and physical effects of stress on controllers."

Controller Staffing:

"1) Accept that the controller workforce is too small and that there are too few experienced controllers. 2) Build a larger, better trained, and much more experienced controller work force. Return supervisors now working as controllers to their supervisory duties."

Traffic Volumes:

"1) Accept that the traffic volume in the ATC system generally exceeds the capabilities of controllers to handle such traffic under conditions of 'normalcy.' 2) Use restrictions to *reduce the volume of traffic* [author's emphasis] until the controller work force, and its experience level, has been matched with the 'normal' capabilities of the controller work force. Allow traffic above this level only as controller numbers and seasoning increases."

This last recommendation is a sore point with the airlines and some of the pilots who fly for them. Despite rampant fare-cutting sparked by deregulation, airlines showed a net profit in 1984 and were expected to do so again in 1985. The gains followed a period from 1981 to 1983 in which red ink flowed in copious quantities. In testimony before Senator Kassebaum's Senate Aviation Subcommittee, Delta Airlines captain Louis McNair spoke on behalf of the Air Line Pilots Association:

"Everyone in the industry agrees that action must be taken to maintain safety in the skies; there is no other acceptable alternative. But there are two options about how to do this. We can reduce—through quotas and flow control and other artificial constraints—the number of aircraft in the sky or we can work to increase the capacity of the system. Frankly, with the economic recovery of the nation and with the airlines poised to recoup terrific losses from the post-deregulation period, it would be a cruel blow to the traveling public and the airlines to arbitrarily re-impose past restrictions. Instead, we must focus all our collective energies into making the system grow while at the same time ensuring no degradation of the margin of safety."

In late 1985, in an effort to expand the system in quantum fashion, seventy-seven members of the House of Representatives signed a letter to President Reagan urging him to rehire 1,000 of the controllers fired in the wake of the PATCO strike. It said, in part: "The problems in our air traffic control system are very real and they are to a point to where passenger safety is being directly affected. We must act now to address the critical problem of controller inexperience."

The lobbying body representing the United States airlines, the Air Transport Association, recommends radical surgery: amputation of air traffic control from the FAA. The result, contends the association, would be a healthy, responsive entity: a federal corporation. Like the Air Line Pilots Association, ATA fears that curtailing traffic could send the industry into a fiscal tailspin. ATA proposes to change the nature of the bureaucracy by redesigning its structure.

In its paper of September 1985, the association reached the following conclusions:

1) "The present FAA structure, with its applicable budget, personnel, and procurement requirements, does not permit effective, business-like decision making and innovative planning of the kind required to operate an ATC system established for the predominant purpose of meeting public demand, and being paid for predominantly by the using public."

2) "No matter how capable the FAA management team may be, the

138

structures and complexities inherent in the present structure result in system management and resource deficiencies that are unlikely to be resolved in any significant way either over the short term or on an ongoing basis without major structural change."

3) "Of several possible structural alternatives, a federal corporation concept offers considerable promise, and could generate needed public and political support under current circumstances (e.g., the deficit problem, efforts to reduce the size of government, and growing popularity of the self-sustaining philosophy for public services)."

4) "Prior studies support transfering ATC system related functions and activities to a federal corporation, and properly designed legislation could assure more effective system management, greater efficiency and cost control, *increased system capacity* [author's emphasis], and quicker response to changing conditions."

ATA believes that a legislative window for making the change will come when Congress begins consideration of the Airport and Airways Improvement Act of 1982, which is due to expire September 30, 1987. Under the ATA proposal, the corporation would be removed from the federal budgetary process. Funding would be provided by users, most prominently the flying public and the airlines. Initial support for the idea on Capitol Hill was mixed. One laconic legislator reminded proponents about the Post Office. In an effort to solve multiple ills, Congress made *it* a federal corporation.

STAYING ALIVE

Aboard Flight 191 was a demographic cross-section of America, brought together in time and space. What they all had in common, with the exception of an infant and two small children, was a boarding pass: a red, white, and blue computer-generated piece of cardboard. In the upper right-hand corner, there's a number, a letter and either the word "Yes" or "No." The space designates seat number, row, and whether the passenger wishes to sit in a smoking or nonsmoking section. On most flights, the pass spells the difference between elbow room and sardine city. On August 2, it meant considerably more.

On impact, the tail of N726DA sheared off on a jagged diagonal. It began just before seat 34J on the right and ended just to the side of 44C on the left. With few exceptions, those behind the line lived and those in front of it died.

Following the crash of 191 and the crash of a Japan Airlines 747SR near Tokyo—in which four survivors were found in the tail—the traveling public adopted the notion that it is invariably safer to sit as far back as possible. For a while, airlines and travel agents reported a small boom in requests for rear seating. Is the tail a haven, or is it some kind of oversized technological talisman? It depends.

Seat selection can make a difference. The problem is that while a rear seat is a lifesaver in many crashes, it's a killer in others. C. O. Miller is an aviation safety consultant and former director of the Bureau of Aviation Safety at the National Transportation Safety Board. His view is that "the tail section does have, in my judgment, a safer position given the total spectrum [of crashes]. But the improvement is so small that I think it's outweighed by other factors," such as cigarette smoke, a bumpy ride, and—with rear-engined jets—noise.

Miller says there are instances in which survival is reduced to elementary physics: "Anytime you have energy absorption during the crash in essentially a fore and aft direction—in other words, the nose of the aircraft hits first and the wings are relatively stable – the breakup forces are going to distribute themselves more severely in the front and become less severe as you go back to the tail."

In findings of probable cause, the NTSB looks at survival aspects separately. Excerpts from some accident reports seem to make a case for rear seaters. In the crash of Air Florida Flight 90 on January 13, 1982, in Washington, D.C. (a Boeing 737), there were six initial survivors: "The only occupiable space in the aircraft that remained intact and not violated by the collapsing cabin structure and furnishings was the rear of the cabin in the vicinity of the aft flight attendant seat."

In the crash of United Flight 73 on December 28, 1978, in Portland, Oregon (a DC-8), there were 171 survivors: "The ten persons who were killed in the crash died from impact trauma." The report went on to say, "The fuselage, from the fifth row of passenger seats forward, sustained severe impact in a generally rearward direction."

Eastern Flight 66, June 24, 1974, JFK: "The fourteen survivors were seated in the inverted rear portion of the passenger cabin. And their seat structures (except for the flight attendant's) also failed. They were less severely injured because the rear portion of the passenger cabin remained relatively intact."

The story is much the same with commuter aircraft in fore-to-aft impact situations. Downeast Airlines Flight 46, May 30, 1979, Rockland, Maine (a DHC-6 Twin Otter), one survivor: "The survival of the one passenger can be attributed to several factors, including . . . his being located far back in the undamaged part of the cabin, which limited the number of dislodged passengers and amount of debris striking him from behind after impact."

Looking at this part of the record, the decison seems clear-cut: aside from the discomfort and other drawbacks of the smoking section, the tail is the place to be. It took the aborted takeoff of a British Airtours 737, twenty days after the crash of 191, to put things in perspective. As the craft roared down the runway at Manchester, England, one of its engines blew. The fuel system then ruptured, dousing the tail. This time, the carnage was in the rear. Those in front escaped. "That's why the back of the aircraft is only safer in certain kinds of accidents," says Miller. "The one factor which, in my judgment, is far more important than the position in the airplane is access to an emergency exit."

A number of accident reports underscore Miller's logic. One in particular is the crash of Pan American Flight 806 on January 30, 1974, in Pago Pago, American Samoa, in which there were five survivors: "This was a survivable accident. The cabin remained intact; the crash forces were within human tolerances; and occupant restraint was maintained throughout the accident. The only traumatic injuries were those to the first officer [copilot]. The survival problems stemmed from post-crash factors. Three major post-crash survival problems were 1) the cabin crew did not open the primary emergency exits, 2) the passenger reaction to the crash, and 3) *passenger inattentiveness to the pre-takeoff briefing and the passenger information pamphlet* (author's emphasis)." Fumes and flame were the killers here.

In the games passengers play, many ignore the preflight safety briefing. This can be especially true of the sophisticated business traveler. The rationale seems to be, "I've flown 50,000-plus miles this year and take the same flight every week. I already *know* where the door is. Briefings are for *in*frequent flyers." Ennui is worn like a badge of rank. Despite the public address pleadings of flight attendants that "even the most seasoned traveler" pay attention, few do.

C. O. Miller maintains that real sophistication, not to mention common sense, demands nothing less than rapt attention to the preflight briefing. Especially important is that card in the seatback pocket, the one with all the red arrows on it. Most people use it as a bookmark for the in-flight magazine. "Every time I get on an airplane – and believe me, I travel frequently – I pick that [safety] card out, read it, and study it. I look at what the bottom of the seats might look like along the aisle, so if necessary I can feel my way along. The point I'm getting at is that even with my knowledge [he helped write many of the cards], I feel it's necessary to refresh my memory every single time that airplane takes off. Even if you're sitting next to an exit, you should look at alternative avenues of escape. You can't depend on any given exit to be available to you, for one reason or another. Either it's damaged, or perhaps there's a fire on that side. You really have to have two routes out."

Statistics show that roughly 80 percent of all crashes are survivable. Your staying alive can depend on your knowledge of available escape options. Mandating those options is the job of the government. Thus, the curious case of the FAA and the 747.

The 747 is a behemoth. In most configurations, it can carry some 440 passengers. In others, such as the 747SR used by Japan Air Lines and All Nippon on routes within the Japanese Archipelago, 550 human beings can be shoe-horned into the aluminum cathedral. The FAA has a formula for determining how many exits are needed to evacuate an airliner successfully in case of emergency: 2 exits per 110 passengers. Based on this theory, the standard 747 (series 100 and 200) requires only 8 escape routes. The formula is predicated on the ability of passengers to get out of a darkened plane within 90 seconds, assuming that half the exits are inoperable. Tests are run to make sure they can.

143

It sounds good, but it's a sham. The tests are conducted using people who know what is about to happen, are prepared for it, and are often employees of the aviation industry. It's similar to fire-drill week at school. You know the bell is going to ring sometime during first period. The flight evacuation criterion is a neatly painted cardboard cutout of what really happens when the interior of an airplane becomes a living hell.

A case in point is Air Canada Flight 797, June 2, 1983, at Greater Cincinnati Airport. The twin-jet DC-9-32 was enroute from DFW to Toronto at flight level 330 (33,000 feet) when fire broke out in an aft lavatory. As smoke and acrid gas began to filter forward, the flight attendants moved passengers to the front of the plane in a space of roughly fifty feet between the front two doors and the overwing exits. Then they began to hand out wet cloths so people could breathe. At the same time, Captain Donald S. Cameron was making an emergency descent into Cincinnati.

The instant the DC-9 stopped its landing roll, flight attendants and passengers threw open two forward doors and three of the four overwing exits. Oxygen rushed into the cabin. In less than ninety seconds, the flammable vapors hovering near the ceiling ignited a deadly phenomenon called "flashover."

The plane was less than half full, with forty-one passengers and five crewmembers. Eighteen passengers and all the crew made it out. Twenty-three others stayed behind. The NTSB said that some of the passengers may have been frozen by fear or incapacitated by toxic hydrogen cyanide and carbon monoxide emitted from the smoldering interior. Some may simply have started for the exits too late or become disoriented. Five exits in a fifty-foot space for forty-one passengers; still, twenty-three dead.

A few months later, with the lessons of Air Canada still theoretically fresh in mind, the Northwest Mountain Region of the FAA bureaucratically blessed the transformation of the 747 into a potential kill jar. Without public notice or comment, the people charged with protecting the flying public whipped out their calculators and decided that the standard 747 really didn't need its existing ten emergency exits. Eight would be just fine. After all, ten escape routes were predicated on maximum usage of the plane: 550 passengers. Only a couple of carriers were doing that. Most configured their jumbos for 440 or less. The FAA made it legal to encapsulate 194 people in a 72-foot space between exits. Without the overwing escapes, a plane would weigh 1,000 pounds less. Less weight meant less fuel and a potentially higher payload. Seats could be placed where the exits used to be. Because of the savings, the passengers in those seats would, theoretically, have to pay less for their tickets.

As of this writing, Boeing has sold more than seventy modification kits to some of the most respected names in international aviation: British Airways, KLM, Cathay Pacific, and C.P. Air among them. "Fortunately," said NTSB chairman Jim Burnett in testimony before the House Subcommittee on Investigations and Oversight, "no U.S. air carriers to our knowledge have acquired these modification kits, and we hope none will do so."

Some charge that the FAA decision was made in virtual secrecy and could violate one of its own rules. In testimony before the subcommittee, Pamela J. Casey of the Association of Flight Attendants said, "We were shocked about this exit removal when it was first casually mentioned at an obscure industry standards meeting." She cited a Federal Air Regulation, FAR 25.803(d), which requires the FAA to conduct a full-scale emergency evacuation demonstration when there is a "major change" in an aircraft. Prior to revising the requirement on the exits, the FAA did not conduct such a demonstration. It chose to rely instead on the formula. A "successful" evacuation had been carried out prior to certificating the 747 for ten exits with a 550-passenger load. That seemed to be all that was required.

NTSB chairman Burnett labeled the FAA ruling a "technical interpretation," adding that the safety board's experience with accident investigation has shown that "the number of exits available in an actual evacuation rarely approaches the theoretically available number mandated by regulations."

Burnett's logic is replete with real-life examples. Perhaps the most dramatic occurred at San Francisco International Airport on July 30, 1971. A Pan American 747 struck some approach lights on takeoff. Steel stakes penetrated the bottom of the fuselage, severely injuring two passengers. The plane was able to waddle into the air, dump excess fuel, and return for an emergency landing. After touchdown, it veered off the right side of the runway. The captain ordered the immediate evacuation of the 197 passengers. During the escape, the nose of the craft tilted up. Two of the forward emergency slides were transformed into little more than vertical shoots as they hung crazily at 68 degrees. Eight people sustained serious back injuries as a result. In addition, four other slides failed to work they way they were supposed to, and a fifth was pinned beneath the fuselage. The 747's ten theoretical escape options had been reduced to just three. Many passengers got out through the overwing exits, the same ones that the FAA decreed were not needed.

This time, the plane did not burn. Passengers were propelled toward useless exits not by poison gas and choking smoke, but by fear of what *might* happen. In opposing the FAA's exit removal, Burnett told the subcommittee, "One can only imagine what would have been the consequences if the fire that had started near the left main landing gear had spread and involved the main fuselage."

In January 1985, in an attempt to get the FAA to reverse itself, the Association of Flight Attendants provided a list of nineteen 747 evacuations where people were killed or injured because of problem exits. That was before an April 25, 1985, incident at Detroit Metro Airport, where a 747 parked at the gate was evacuated because the crew thought there was a fire. Since they were at the gate, only six exits were tried. Half of them worked the way they should have.

Bowing to public and congressional pressure, the agency asked—did not tell—the airlines to keep the unneeded exits, anyway. Consumer advocate Ralph Nader

145

accused the federal officials of legal blame-shifting when he told the subcommittee: "According to the FAA, removing the exits would violate the carrier's duty under the Federal Aviation Act to provide the highest possible degree of safety." As of this writing, the agency was reviewing the wisdom of permitting the reduction in the first place.

The adage, "It's the smoke that kills you, not the fire," is especially true of otherwise survivable airplane crashes. In the aftermath of the Air Canada crash, blood samples were taken from both the living and the dead. They were analyzed at the FAA's Civil Aeromedical Institute at Oklahoma City. The findings surprised virtually no one. According to the NTSB accident report, "The results of the analyses indicated that the deceased had elevated carbon monoxide levels ranging from 20 to 63 percent saturation; the threshold for carbon monoxide in the blood at which incapacitation occurs is between 40 and 50 percent saturation. The cyanide levels found in the blood samples of the deceased ranged from a low of 0.8 to a high of 5.12 micrograms/ml; the toxic level for cyanide in the blood at which incapacitation occurs is between 0.5 and 0.7 micrograms/ml."

Those who died on Flight 797 breathed in an acidic witches' brew of hydrogen chloride, hydrogen fluoride, and hydrogen cyanide. Topping off this hellish concoction was carbon monoxide. The gasses were thrown off as fire progressively consumed the lavatory walls, propagated into the ceiling, and moved inexorably forward. By the time Captain Cameron braked the DC-9 to a halt, the smoke was so thick that visibility was vitually nonexistent a couple of feet above the floor.

One of the airlines' biggest selling points today, especially to business travelers, is the availability of overhead storage for carry-on luggage. Baggage lines are anathema to most fast-moving frequent flyers. But when ignited, those cool earthtone plastics and pretty pastel fabrics that decorate an airliner's interior become poison producers. The handy overhead compartment above your seat is transformed into a deadly pandora's box as plastics, polyesters, and pantyhose melt, fuse, and vent their poison into the air. Even that favorite wool overcoat carefully stored each summer is potentially deadly. It can emit enough cyanide to kill seven people.

146

There were those in the aviation community who considered Air Canada 797 as much travesty as tragedy. What happened at Cincinnati was a carbon monoxide copy of Paris ten years earlier. On July 11, 1973, a Varig Boeing 707 crash-landed at Paris after a lavatory fire. One hundred twenty-four people died. In the wake of the investigation, the NTSB recommended that the FAA require oxygen bottles and full face masks for each flight attendant so they could better combat on-board fires. Ten years later, the issue was still pending. It was not until October 1985 that the agency finally issued a Notice of Proposed Rule Making (NPRM), the first step toward addressing the problem.

Even should a rule requiring breathing units for flight attendants finally be adopted, it appears that passengers will still have to make do with wet washcloths or cocktail napkins soaked in their favorite mixer. In 1970 the FAA withdrew an NPRM that could have led to smoke hoods for passengers.

Former Congressman Elliot Levitas, while chairman of the House Sub-committee on Investigations and Oversight, called the withdrawal part of "a sorry chronology of neglect" by the FAA of significant improvements in cabin safety. John Galipault, president of the Aviation Safety Institute, says, "We should be providing an effective smoke hood for every person on the airplane, not just the crew." He advocates replacing the "Mickey Mouse" overhead oxygen masks that are now standard on commercial jets with hoods "that supply oxygen on demand" to passengers using them. A quick-disconnect device would enable passengers to escape a burning plane "with a minute or two of breathable oxygen" trapped in the hood. He says that such a hood, manufactured by DuPont, is already a reality.

The FAA claims that hoods would cost lives, not save them. Tests conducted at the Civil Aeromedical Institute, officials say, prove that donning the devices increases evacuation time in darkness by 50 percent. "Everything we've done in our research has told us the best thing to do is to get people trained to get out of the airplane fast," says Tom McSweeney, manager for aircraft engineering of the agency's division of airworthiness. How rapid retreat from a burning airplane reconciles with permitting removal of 747 window exits is another matter.

The FAA has known since 1961 that passengers who survived the actual impact of a crash often died as a result of breathing deadly gasses. It took the Air Canada crash, and the congressional firestorm that it ignited, to spur the agency to action. In October 1984 the FAA finally acted on some of NTSB's long-standing recommendations involving cabin safety: By November 26, 1987, aircraft seat cushions have to meet improved flammability standards. By November 26, 1986, the nation's airliners have to be equipped with lighted "floor proximity emergency escape paths," which point the way out. By October 29, 1986, the lavatories of airliners must be equipped with smoke detectors. By April 29, 1987, automatic fire extinguishers have to be in place in lavatory trash receptacles. Additional hand-held fire extinguishers, two of which contain Halon extinguishing agent, were to have been in place by **147** April 29, 1986.

Still, many FAA critics, such as Nader's Aviation Consumer Action Project, maintain that the agency did not go far enough—that it did not attack one of the causes of the problem. They feel that strict limits should be set on the volume of smoke and gasses that cabin materials are permitted to emit.

The FAA has countered, in effect, by saying that where there's smoke, there's fire—that it's the flammability issue that is pivotal. The agency contends that lethal doses of gasses are not emitted until actual cabin flashover occurs. Reduce the chance of that occurring, and smoke and gas toxicity standards become moot. The agency is quick to point to the new rule mandating that fire-blocking layers be installed between the highly flammable polyurethane foam cushions used in aircraft seats. As noted above, airliners must have the new cushions by late 1987. The agency is not as eager to refer to some of the results of an $11.8 million test conducted in late 1984 whose major goal was to test something called AMK. AntiMisting Kerosene was touted as a lifesaving elixir, a fuel additive that would virtually eliminate the massive fireball that often erupts when an airplane crashes. One FAA official labeled it "the most important product ever to come down the pike for fire safety in airplanes."

Normally, jet fuel is not especially volatile. Drop a lighted match into a container of the stuff, and there's no fire. But in a crash, the liquid that spews from ruptured fuel tanks is turned into a fine, highly flammable mist. The tiniest spark can trigger an inferno. The FAA says that 40 percent of postcrash fire fatalities are attributable to fuel misting.

What AMK does is make fuel molecules adhere to one another rather than mist. That's fine for reducing volatility, but it produces problems in the plane's power plants. Fuel has to mist before jet engines can work. The problem was solved by installing a mechanism that degrades the additive just before fuel is fed to the engine.

In-flight tests confirmed that AMK-hyped fuel could indeed power a jetliner with no appreciable problems. Initial tests of AMK at the FAA's Technical Center in Atlantic City were also promising. When an old navy patrol craft was slammed into obstructions, fuel tanks ruptured right on cue. There was fire, but no fireball. The next step would be the clincher, confirming what many industry observers were already taking as gospel. On December 1, 1984, a remotely piloted, four-engine Boeing 720 (a slightly smaller version of the venerable 707) took off for a rehearsed rendezvous with disaster. In its tanks were 12,000 gallons of AMK-laced additive. The craft's complement of passengers consisted of seventy-five lifelike mannequins—high-tech replicas of men, women, and children who would feel no pain, leave no families, and "die" with blank expressions on their faces should things go awry. In lieu of an in-flight movie, the passengers themselves were the show. Their movements would be monitored by an array of high-speed cameras. Some 350 sensing devices would record what happened when the doomsday flight kissed the California desert and then impaled itself on a mine field of metal.

Even in mock disasters, things don't always go as expected. Just before touchdown, something happened. The nose pitched down as the wings began to roll. The left wing hit the ground first, 281 feet short of target. In a scenario not unlike that of Delta 191, the nose of the plane slewed left. For 1,400 feet the massive jet kicked up a rooster tail of dust as it skittered across the desert. Suddenly, the dust was replaced with something else: a thick pall of black smoke, the ugly thumbprint of a fireball.

Fire fighters extinguished the charred remains more than an hour later. So intense was the fire that it melted large holes in the aluminum skin of the fuselage. Had people – not dummies – been sitting in those seats, the crash would have been, in bureaucratic parlance, "nonsurvivable."

Nine months later the FAA quietly shelved AMK. Said FAA administrator Donald Engen in a letter to the House Public Works and Transportation Committee's Aviation Subcommittee: "The failure mode highlighted by the controlled impact demonstration and other technical issues not yet resolved lead me to conclude that the concept is not practical for day-to-day airline operation in the foreseeable future."

The test was far from being the waste of money the media initially portrayed it as being. Valuable information was collected on crash survival. All that remains to be done is for government to translate lessons into lifesaving practice.

A handful of intellectuals, designers, and entrepreneurs contend that the aviation establishment approaches safety symptomatically. They argue that a radical, *fundamental* change is needed in aircraft design philosophy. Ironically, an example of such a craft may be cloistered in a Connecticut museum. The CBY-3 was the last creation of Vincent Justice Burnelli, a maverick aeronautical engineer from Texas. His wide, squat-looking plane isn't pretty. Yet it is the ugly-duckling appearance that – proponents say – makes the design both safe and efficient. It all goes back to lift. Burnelli's genius lay in designing an airplane whose fuselage itself contributes to flight: a "lifting body." Conventional aircraft, especially today's jet transports, have long, cigar-shaped fuselages. They sacrifice lift for speed. Cylindrical designs produce "parasite drag," a phenomenon constantly at war with lift.

Burnelli died in 1964. For eighteen years his plans gathered dust. Then, in the spring of 1982, two men resurrected the historical oddity. One of them was Chalmers "Slick" Goodlin, the man who piloted the famed X-1 rocket plane in its initial tests, the ones that preceded Chuck Yeager's successful lancing of the sound barrier. Goodlin had met Burnelli shortly after piloting the X-1. The two agreed that the supersonic craft exemplified the problem of parasite drag: enormous thrust was required to overcome the virtual deadweight of the fuselage. Test pilot and designer became lifelong friends.

149

The rejuvenated Burnelli Company has recently courted European and Japanese manufacturers in efforts to launch a modern jet prototype of the lifting body concept. Goodlin says that there has been some "real interest. More and more, the traveling public and governments are realizing that we have to have a more efficient and safer plane."

Traditional passenger jets, despite their array of lift-enhancing devices like flaps and slats, still require relatively long runways. Takeoffs and landings are the most critical periods of any flight—high-speed affairs that can tax the limits of man and machine. Margins for error are microscopic.

After a DC-8 accident in Denver, the Air Line Pilots Association wrote the FAA asking that more work be done to lower critical takeoff and landing speeds: "This Association conducts evaluations of new airline aircraft and, in this regard, we have had the opportunity of doing some design and flight evaluation of an aircraft which approaches the flying wing concept. We refer to the Burnelli transport. We were favorably impressed with its design features which permit slow flight with high gross weight, considering the low horsepower. The design of this airplane also permits considerable in-flight inspection of the control systems, powerplants and landing gear. The advantage of this is obvious from a safety standpoint." ALPA asked the FAA to consider an updated version of the Burnelli.

Years later, FAA spokesman Dennis Feldman said the agency had not tested the Burnelli concept. "We certificate new aircraft to see that they meet certain criteria as far as performance is concerned." Encouraging manufacturers to explore the Burnelli design "is not our function."

Says Goodlin, "Engineering and executive thinking alike seem to have been afflicted with a form of psychological inertia which allows them to pursue only the easy way of getting designs done—that of laying next year's requirements over last year's airplane."

There is sentiment in the aviation community that the "old ways" are not working too well. The prestigious British publication *Flight International* has questioned whether "we're looking at things the right way" and editorially called for a fundamental reassessment of "the requirements for total air safety, from basic aircraft design upwards"—which brings us back to Vincent Burnelli's dream.

His prototype UB-14 crashed near Newark Airport on January 13, 1935, due to faulty maintenance. What should have been disaster turned to triumph. The pilot was Louis T. Reichers, who would eventually become chief of the Air Transport Command's engineering section. He said, "The indicated airspeed (IAS) was 195 at the time it became essential for me to make a crash landing. I flew the ship into the ground from about 200 ft. altitude and the estimated speed of contact was about 130 m.p.h., with the right wing being nearly vertical and absorbing the first shock. The impact caused the aircraft to cartwheel, tearing off the engines and crushing the wings and tail group, with the body tumbling throughout but remaining intact. No fuel leaked from the wings. It is my firm belief that the box-body strength of this type, combined with the engines forward and the landing gear retracted, saved myself and the engineering crew. Also, *had the cabin been fully occupied with passengers with safety belts properly attached, no passengers would have been injured* [author's emphasis]. This crash landing, in my opinion, is an extraordinary example of the crash safety that can be provided by the lifting body design."

Wind tunnel and computer tests of the Burnelli are tantalizing. In addition to being demonstrably safer than conventional aircraft, the plane is less expensive to operate, according to Goodlin. The lifting body actually becomes more aerodynamically efficient as its speed and size increase. More lift combined with less drag equals smaller power plants and reduced fuel consumption.

On the first day of March 1978, a Continental Airlines DC-10 lumbered onto a rain-stained Runway 6 Right at Los Angeles International Airport. At 430,000 pounds, the huge widebody flirted with its maximum takeoff weight. As the jet hurtled along, approaching a V1 speed of 156 knots—the point at which the pilot decides to abort or continue takeoff—something went terribly wrong. There was a loud bang: a retreaded tire had succumbed to weight, friction, and the laws of centrifugal force. The other three tires on the left main landing gear failed in sickening sequence. The DC-10, despite the best efforts of the crew, was doomed. The pilot pushed down hard on the left rudder pedal, avoiding a bank of approach lights. The plane had slowed to sixty-eight miles per hour when it left the runway. The left main gear broke through the concrete and ruptured a fuel tank. Fire broke out. Two people died that day, and thirty-one others were injured escaping the inferno.

It didn't have to happen. A Burnelli jet transport would never have reached such high takeoff speeds. Even if there had been an accident, it is likely that the devastating fire would never have erupted and that the passengers would have escaped unscathed.

Professor Edmund J. Cantelli is an aviation safety expert at the Polytechnic Institute of New York. He notes that in many current commercial jets, landing gear and engines are attached to structures that support fuel tanks. "It's easy to see," say Cantelli, "why airplane crashes often end in flames." In the proposed Burnelli jet, the gear would be attached to the box-like passenger assembly itself, the strongest part of the aircraft structure. The fuel tanks would be in the wings, away from the cabin. Should quick evacuation be necessary, Burnelli passengers would not have to contend with long slides down vulnerable escape chutes; they would simply step out of the low-slung cabin to the ground.

In the early 1970s, a jet-powered lifting body transport almost made it from the drawing board to the real world. It was called the "Husky" and was a collaborative study involving a group formed by former General Motors boss Ed Cole and the Boeing Commercial Airplane Company. The design of the cargo-carrying craft, which was big enough to support a veritable parking lot of vehicles, looked promising. Even though the focus was on packages instead of people, the aviation community seemed to be ready for something really new. What happened?

The driving force behind the project, Ed Cole, died. In addition, Boeing

151

spokesman Tom Cole (no relation) says the projected growth in air freight just hasn't materialized: "Until air freight gets to be a more significant part of the world's economy, a fleet of great freighters like that isn't going to work." The Boeing spokesman calls the lifting body proposed by the former GM chief "a grand scheme a little ahead of its time, I think."

It could be that Vincent Burnelli was also "ahead of his time." His airplanes were elegantly ugly in their first incarnations. Yet neither they nor their sleek, stillborn progeny have really ever had a chance. Considering commercial aviation's recent record, maybe it's time they did.

EPILOGUE

Official statistics don't reflect it, but Delta 191 took 138, not 137, lives. On Thanksgiving Day, 1985, Frances Christy, Kathy Ford's mother, died unexpectedly at age sixty-one. Following the crash, she—along with daughter Carol and son-in-law Terry—kept virtually constant vigil beside Kathy's bedside. The unrelenting strain took its toll. Frances Christy's heart literally broke.

Johnny Meier, the man who loved window seats, has not been on an airplane since August 2. He still has dreams about that evening. "I really don't want to fly," he says. "I'm scared."

Some attorneys predict that federal lawsuits stemming from the crash could eventually number a hundred or more. Not included in the count is one lodged in Texas State Court; it's against the estate of Edward M. Connors.

In addition to its papers against the FAA, Delta contemplated legal action of a different kind. In its rush to get loved ones to DFW, the airline flew in a Florida man who said he was the fiance of a woman passenger. After he checked into the Hilton, it was discovered that he was an imposter.

The twenty thousand or so pieces of mail carried aboard Flight 191 have skyrocketed in value. After the crash, postal workers separated, dried, and stored the cards and letters. Then they stamped the charred, mottled paper with a purple message: "DAMAGED IN AIR, MAIL, TRUCK OR SHIP ACCIDENT. BEYOND CONTROL OF THE U.S. POSTAL SERVICE." Some of the addressees who received the effluent decided to sell it to collectors. The going price is $10 for a standard letter-sized envelope.

There has been a change at the National Weather Service's Fort Worth Forecast Office. "Everyone is running scared," said one employee. Now, when an echo appears near the airport, people pick up the phone to the DFW tower.

The FAA has apparently taken definitive action. The city of Irving's plans

153

to develop an eighty-seven-acre park in the approach zone to DFW were scuttled by the crash. The mayor said he was told the agency "didn't like the idea anymore. They were worried about the risk factor of a park being too close to the runway."

Finally, a curious occurrence, one of those things that can never be touched on in any official recounting. Just before 191 turned on final approach to Runway 17 Left, more than a thousand miles away in South Florida, Marilyn Steinberg's intricate depiction of flight was being crated. Next stop: exhibition. As the framer picked it up to slide it in its box, the frame holding "Upward Bound" unaccountably started to shake, rattling with some primal power. Moments later, it shattered.

INDEX

157

Texas State Fair, 43
Third-party complaint, 80
TOGA (take off go around), 16
Toxic gas, 144, 146
TRACON, 121–122, 126, 134–135. *See* Traffic Control.
Traffic Control, 121. *See* TRACON.
Traffic volume, 135, 139
Trailing edge, 9, 104
Transponder, 8
Trauma Center, 38. *See also* Parkland Hospital.
Triage, 35
TriStar, 5, 108. *See* Lockheed L1011 TriStar.
Turkish DC-10, 79

UB-14, 150
Unions, 90
United Airlines, 109
United Airlines Flight 73, 142
United States Aviation Underwriters, 61, 73. *See* USAIG.
United States Supreme Court, 81
University of Chicago, 103
University of Texas Health Science Center, 31, 36, 38, 86
"Upward Bound", 11, 154
USAIG, 66, 74–76. *See* United States Aviation Underwriters.

Varig Airlines Boeing 707, 81
Vee R, 106. *See* VR.
Vee two, 107. *See* V2.
Very-High-Frequency Omni-Directional radio-range navigational station, 8
Visual Flight Rules, 134. *See* VFR.
Vortex, 108

Vortex curl, 104, 107, 113

Wade, Henry, 72
Walter, Pam, 39–40
Washington Post, 117
Water tanks, 17, 45, 123
Wayson, Thomas, 12
Weiland Funeral Directors, 66
White, Annie, 29–30, 33
White, Dana, 29, 33
White, Leora, 29–33
White, Mark, 73
White, Ron, 29–33
Williams, Jack, 14
Wind shear, 3, 103, 105, 107–114
Wind shear detection devices, 113–114
Wind Shear Warning/Recovery Guidance System (WSW/RG), 114
Work-life expectancy, 77
Wrongful-death statute (California), 79
WSW/RG, 114. *See* Wind Shear Warning/Recovery Guidance System.

Yoke, 109, 113